FUTURE WEAPONS

ACCESS GRANTED

ALLISON BARRIE

ARBUTHNOT & TREVELYAN
LONDON

Arbuthnot & Trevelyan
Isle of Skye - London
www.arbuthnottrevelyan.com

For information about special discounts and bulk purchases please contact sales@arbuthnottrevelyan.com. For details on special discounts for quantity purchases by corporations, associations, organizations and universities contact the publisher at business@arbuthnottrevelyan.com.

Cover and book design by Ebook Launch

Printed in the United States of America

Library of Congress Cataloging-in-Publication Data has been applied for:
Barrie, Allison.
Future Weapons: Access Granted / Allison Barrie. – 1st ed.
p. cm.
ISBN 978-0-9976734-0-1/ 978-0-9976734-1-8

First Edition

14 13 12 11 10 / 10 9 8 7 6 5 4 3 2

Contents

INTRODUCTION

Invisible tanks. Drone swarms. Railguns slinging Mach 6 slugs. Terminator-style robot troops and cyborg fighters. Space-based lasers blasting apocalyptic threats. Hand-launched micro missiles. Next-gen mega stealth bombers traveling an entire continent in mere minutes....Sound like the stuff of science fiction? Just a few examples of the very real military tech in development and explained in *Future Weapons: Access Granted.*

In this book, you'll find an insider's guide to the latest remarkable advances underway that could shape battles to come. I travel around the world searching for game-changing breakthroughs. Frequently, I get to explore the most elite government and commercial installations, where shrouded in utmost secrecy behind heavily fortified walls, they make the most cutting-edge innovations for war. And I don't just look at this future tech—I regularly get to test it out and kick those next-gen tires. I'm excited to share my unique access with you and you'll find it leveraged to the hilt in this book.

Over the years, I've looked at thousands of advances and often I'm invited to reveal them first to the public. You may have seen my reporting on them on my website, in my column carried in places like foxnews.com as FOX Firepower, or you may have seen me on television channels around the world talking about them.

I've curated for you some of my favorites that I've covered over the years. It was no easy task trying to narrow it down from thousands and thousands to about

100 (with a few more I just couldn't resist including). How did I choose when there are so many amazing advances I've been so very lucky to see? Some are favorites for the fearless imagination and determination the teams demonstrated to make what others believe impossible—possible. Some are favorites because I believe they will be vital to ensure matching, if not overmatching, adversaries in future combat. Some are favorites because it is incredibly good fun driving, flying or firing them. And many were chosen for being a combination of the three.

All of them I find just plain fascinating and I hope you do too. When possible I've updated the stories and added more detail for you. I've also peppered in some inside scoop on a few of my experiences exploring and testing out these extraordinary advances.

So what will you find inside? The book is organized into five broad themes: weapons, land, maritime, air and unmanned. The first section dives into future weapons starting with electromagnetic railguns and followed by directed energy (aka lasers), electronic warfare, classics and enhanced classics. It closes with some innovations in, and for, handheld weapons.

The next section is dedicated to land advances where you can discover more about new armored vehicles and then some fast and light tactical options favored by special operations forces. After this, you'll find innovation that could help pave the way for what could eventually become future ground troops: robots and cyborgs.

The third section focuses on maritime and looks at advances underwater, small and fast options designed with special operations in mind, and then gives you some ideas about what could be next in surface combat.

In the following air section, you can explore the latest fighters, stealth bombers, helicopters, enhanced classics and out of the box concepts.

The final section of the book dips into some new unmanned platforms and introduces a few future micro and extended reach and range solutions. This section closes by touching on some potential extreme ISR and strike capabilities. I prefer the term unmanned or Unmanned Autonomous Vehicle (UAV, UUV etc.), but I understand media has popularized the term "drone." Since it has become familiar shorthand for folks, I've used the term drone here too, for your ease of reference.

This book is dedicated to the Great Escape Fifty who alongside their fellow prisoners did so very much with so very little. The prisoners have long had my admiration for refusing to the let the enemy defeat them; and instead with relentless ingenuity, determination and team work, those captured dauntlessly devised ways to improvise, to escape and to return to the fight.

I'd also like to take this opportunity to thank all the trailblazing teams who created and nurtured the tech reviewed in this book. Always such a privilege to learn about your work, always such an honor to visit, explore and try out your advances and always humbled by your dedication to providing the U.S. military and its allies with the very best in the world.

From Predator-style chameleon armor that disappears into its surroundings through to Transformer-type assault vehicles... get ready to dive into some of the latest, greatest and most exciting advances for future combat.

FUTURE WEAPONS
ACCESS GRANTED

WEAPONS

ELECTROMAGNETIC RAILGUNS

EM RAILGUNS

The U.S. military continues to lead the charge on a weapon that seems so futuristic that many naysayers love to say it is impossible. And yet, the Electromagnetic Railgun has already proven them wrong. It isn't just possible—tests have proven that railguns are achievable and can unleash extreme effects.

In the not so distant future, railguns could fire projectiles that will strike enemy targets at speeds faster than Mach 6—that's a remarkable six times the speed of sound. In fact in recent trials, projectiles already exited the muzzle at 4500 miles an hour—that's more than a mile a second. Once combat ready, it is expected a ship could carry thousands of railgun projectiles and the weapon could fire a devastating ten rounds a minute.

The Electromagnetic Railgun has the potential to revolutionize naval warfare and the Navy continues to push innovation in this arena. Both General Atomics and BAE Systems have been working on next generation prototype EM Railguns to arm the future fleet.

How does it work?

No gunpowder. No explosives.

An EM Railgun is a long-range weapon that uses electromagnetic energy, instead of conventional chemical propellants, to fire projectiles.

Railguns launch these projectiles using electromagnetic forces. The projectiles harness the kinetic energy from the extreme velocity. The muzzle velocity of a railgun can be more than twice that of conventional weapons.

This weapon requires a great deal of power to generate the electromagnetic forces. In a naval setting, for example, a ship would generate electricity and store it in a pulsed power system. An electric pulse is sent to it the railgun where an electromagnetic force is created. The force accelerates the projectile and launches it between two conductive rails at extreme speeds. By adjusting the electromagnetic pulse, the range can be varied.

The weapon gets its name from its use of rails. High electrical currents accelerate a sliding metal conductor between two rails and this creates magnetic fields to launch projectiles.

Once launched, the projectile harvests extreme speed for maximum effect. In some recent tests, a 25-pound projectile tore through seven steel plates and left a five-inch hole.

Faster than a bullet: Extreme speed and range

The electromagnetic force is so powerful that it slings the projectile at speeds up to about Mach 6—this is faster and farther than current options. In recent tests, these projectiles have reached an amazing 4,500 mph and precisely hit targets more than 100 miles away.

Once launched, the projectile uses its extreme speed — the kinetic energy rather than conventional explosives — to destroy targets on land, at sea or in the air.

To put this extreme speed into context, railgun projectiles travel at a whopping six times the speed of sound. So how fast is that? The average bullet travels about 1,700 miles per hour—so a railgun projectile can travel more than two and half times faster than the typical bullet.

And to put the improved distance in perspective, the current five inch 62-caliber Mk 45 Mod 4 naval gun system has a range of about 23 miles with the new 5-inch Cargo projectile. The railgun could have a range of 125 miles—that gives the Navy approximately 110 miles more range. Railguns mean remarkably extended range.

And ultimately the railguns may be able to hit targets more than 150 miles away in about two minutes. The speed, range, effect and precision are all great advantages. Research and development could lead to providing the U.S. military with even more velocity and further range.

How would a Railgun be used?

The EM Railgun is one immensely powerful weapon. Railgun-armed ships will be able to fire hypervelocity projectiles giving U.S. forces this even greater reach and lethality. The weapons could be deployed against a spectrum of threats for precision strikes against targets on land, at sea or in the air.

So what sort of damage can it actually do? A potent offensive weapon, it could tear holes in enemy ships and destroy heavily fortified enemy command centers to name just a few examples. It would bring a serious amount of additional firepower for surface warfare and in support of U.S. Marines and ground forces. The railgun also could be employed defensively to protect ships.

The Navy has been considering arming the new *Zumwalt*-class and other ships with the weapon. But lots of development is also underway for railgun applications beyond ships.

Advantage U.S. Navy

Railguns are a smart alternative to current large artillery and could represent a significant advance in Navy and Marine Corps capabilities. In addition to enhancing precision strikes, railguns offer a number of other advantages.

The magazine is deep. It will only be limited by factors like the ship's power and cooling capacity. The weapon could also provide benefits like enhancing safety aboard surface ships, while greatly reducing cost.

Taking the safety issue first...Since this system does not use gunpowder or propellant to fire the projectile, it reduces the need for high explosives to be carried on ships and the related hazards in doing so. Off the ship, the EM Railgun will improve safety as well. Since it uses its extreme speed on impact, the danger of unexploded ordnance on the battlefield would be reduced.

Another key advantage is cost. Railgun projectiles are a mere fraction of the cost of those currently used in missile engagements. In theory, railgun projectiles could tackle the same threats, at the same range, even more effectively—and do so for a much smaller price tag per shot.

EM RAILGUN PROJECTILES

So what does this futuristic weapon fire? A railgun needs ammo—and it can't just lob traditional options. Even the ammunition for the railgun has had to be revolutionary.

Inside the General Atomics projectile, there are navigation sensors and processors for guidance, navigation and control. Within the launcher, the projectiles withstand a multi-Tesla magnetic field. The three-mega joule Blitzer electromagnetic railgun system fired five test projectiles at accelerations greater than 30,000 times that of gravity in recent tests. General Atomics has announced they've performed very successfully.

BAE Systems is developing the HVP or Hyper Velocity Projectile to be fired by the Navy's EM Railgun and future models of railguns. The HVP will also be compatible with current weapons systems like the Navy 5-Inch Mk 45, and Navy, Marine Corps, and Army 155-mm Tube Artillery systems.

It's designed to be a guided projectile with low drag for high-velocity, maneuverability and decreased time-to-target. HVP has advanced guidance electronics. The flight body is 24 inches long and it weighs about 28 pounds. The integrated launch package is 12 pounds heavier and two inches longer, so the projectiles will be easy to handle and transport.

The Navy's EM Railgun could ultimately fire 10 of these rounds per minute. When fired with an Mk 45, the HVP could be 20 rounds per minute and extend range to 50 nautical miles.

Making railguns a reality

Achieving this *Star Wars*-style weapon has not been easy. For years, many programs have sought to build such a powerful weapon, but a design that works—and works on a practical level—has been incredibly difficult to crack. Generating the power alone that's necessary to accelerate railgun projectiles has been just one big challenge. And creating materials capable of resisting the extreme temperatures generated by it has been another fundamental one.

Development of Office of Naval Research's Electromagnetic Railgun began about ten years ago. The first phase focused on developing the launcher, pulsed power, and risk reduction for the projectile. In 2012, the second phase began further advancing the tech and working on aspects like a firing rate of 10 rounds per minute. In September 2014, the Office of Naval Research (ONR) and Naval Sea Systems Command (NAVSEA) fired a high velocity projectile during a successful test held at the Naval Surface Warfare Center Dahlgren Division.

In 2015, military tests showed that by using railgun projectiles in conventional guns that the range could be extended. During tests that fired 5- and 6-inch Navy guns loaded with a version of the railgun projectile, the 6-inch gun range was reportedly extended from 15 miles to 38 miles. In the 155mm Army howitzers, the range was also extended by using the railgun projectiles.

In 2016, General Atomics Electromagnetic Systems announced that its Blitzer railgun hypersonic projectiles successfully passed open-range tests at the U.S. Army Dugway Proving Ground in Utah.

The Navy continues to forge ahead turning something once of science fiction into a formidable weapon for future combat. Both General Atomics and BAE Systems have continued to develop their next gen EM Railguns. The railgun program continues to perform impressively and make headway. In a key next step for railgun development, the Navy announced it would be testing the technology at sea in 2016.

DIRECTED ENERGY

CLWS - the Drone Slayer

A revolution is afoot to arm the U.S. military with directed energy weapons – that's lasers big and small. Lasers don't run out of ammunition. Provided they've got power, they can keep on delivering focused firepower. And given laser beams work at the speed of light, theoretically it is very difficult, if not impossible, for targets to dodge a laser beam.

Invisible and silent...Boeing's new laser cannon slays enemy drones by taking them down in under a minute. This first laser, the Compact Laser Weapons System (CLWS), is an example of the quest to make man carried lasers a reality.

CLWS is a lighter, smaller, easily transportable version of Boeing's powerful High Energy Laser Mobile Demonstrator. This two kilowatt system is small enough to be carried (no small feat for laser systems which tend to be very heavy and very large) and it assembles rapidly in mere minutes. It's not nearly handheld, but the system can be broken down into four parts and each part takes one or two warfighters to transport it. In total, the system weighs about 650 pounds - that's very light for lasers.

In spite of it diminutive size compared to other systems, it is powerful enough to do some serious damage. CLWS can destroy targets beyond 22 miles away and can defeat enemy drones in mere seconds.

In tests at Port Mugu in 2015, Boeing demonstrated what the tech could do. With precision, the directed energy rapidly burned holes in "enemy" drones, forcing them to crash. The directed energy was focused on a spot to heat it up and damage the target. Thus far, the precision is such that the laser can zero in on a very small drone's tail and within 10 to 15 seconds succeed in setting it on fire.

Directed energy beams, by their very nature, are silent and invisible. What does it feel like to be struck by a laser beam like CLWS? It has been described to me as being blasted by an invisible welding torch. You wouldn't be able to identify the source or even understand what is happening to you. Not something an adversary would be keen to experience I'd imagine.

How does it work?

The CLWS is a two-kilowatt laser that focuses a directed energy beam at a target. It's so precise it can even target a specific location on a very small drone. The target does not need to be stationary. The system can identify and track air and ground targets as they are moving. It does this using a mid-wave infrared sensor and it has a range of about 40 kilometers.

It takes just one warfighter to operate the laser, directing it with an Xbox 360-like controller connected to a laptop equipped with the targeting software. The system is designed to be portable so it takes just a few boxes and a few warfighters to move the laser around the battlespace. The laser can be set up and ready to go in minutes to deliver some focused firepower.

CLWS is sort of a little brother to Boeing's 10 kilowatt laser HEL MD. The High Energy Laser Mobile Demonstrator (discussed later in this book's *Weapons* section) is Boeing's laser that is mounted on a truck and can destroy mortars while they are in mid-flight. CLWS is smaller and man-portable variant.

How would it be used?

The CLWS could be used to defeat drone threats in war zones, but also in the U.S. to protect and defend sensitive areas. From hobbyists through to companies like Amazon, drone use in the U.S. has widely proliferated. As just one illustration of this sort of threat, a man was arrested for flying a drone near the White House in 2015. Places like airports and government buildings continue to be targeted by drones. Security experts are concerned that a drone could carry threats like explosives or biological and chemical weapons. Small drones could also be used for surveillance and to gather intelligence near sensitive, government areas. A weapon like CLWS could prove very useful to defeat these sorts of small drone threats.

ADAM – the Boat Blaster

Made by Lockheed Martin, ADAM, or Area Defense Anti-Munitions, is another laser weapon system currently at a smaller scale and aimed at being portable. But in addition to land, ADAM is specifically designed to provide this capability at sea too.

ADAM can take out military grade small boats, close-in improvised rockets and drones. From forward operating bases through to ships, it could be used to protect a range of things. It has been tested as a 10 kilowatt, single-mode fiber laser weapon system, with a view to scaling up. The portable system continues to evolve, but currently it can track moving targets at a range of more than 5 kilometers and to destroy threats at up to about 2 kilometers.

How does it work?

This directed energy weapon system detects a threat and within seconds locks on to the target. It establishes an aim point. Once ADAM declares valid aim point, the system fires the laser on the target long enough to neutralize the threat whether it's a hostile small boat, drone or rocket.

ADAM took out two boats at a range of about a mile way in a 2014 field test. It has been able to track and blast targets up to about three miles away and was able to burn through rubber hulls of the military grade boats in 30 seconds. ADAM also previously proved successful at taking out targets in flight as well. Its laser beam has blasted threats like drones and rockets.

GBAD – Tactical Vehicle Laser Weapon

Mount a laser weapon on a tactical vehicle and you've got directed energy on demand to rapidly smite large unmanned systems and other threats you may come across.

The Navy hasn't just been extremely forward leaning developing breakthroughs in the futuristic railguns, the Navy is also rapidly advancing lasers as well.

The Office of Naval Research has a laser weapon underway that will be able to shoot down big armed and ISR drones, spelling big trouble for any enemy who tries to target the U.S. military—and particularly expeditionary forces operating on land.

GBAD—Ground-Based Air Defense Directed Energy On-the-Move—is a laser weapon that could be installed on Humvees, Joint Light Tactical Vehicles and other light tactical ground vehicles. In addition to providing an affordable alternative to traditional firepower, GBADs could prevent enemy drones from tracking and targeting Marines on the ground.

The system

Some of the system's components had already been used in tests to detect and track a range of unmanned aerial vehicles. But the fundamental challenge is to create a powerful laser weapon that is light enough to carry on light tactical vehicles without affecting the vehicle's speed and agility. Directed energy weapons require a lot of power—so GBADs will need to crack how to provide that on a light vehicle too.

The 30-kilowatt laser system includes the cannon part (aka beam director), cooling hardware and lithium-ion batteries for power-storage—all in a way that makes sense for a tactical vehicle.

In the near term, it may require three vehicles. One laser-mounted vehicle would work together with another that carries a radar and a third equipped with the computerized control system. As a team, the three systems and crews work together to detect, track, and destroy threats.

ONR is working with the Naval Surface Warfare Center Dahlgren Division and industry partners to develop the laser, radar and beam director. They're also collaborating to create advanced cooling, communications, batteries and more.

Next level Avengers

The Marines could have new amped up capabilities in their very near future—a mere five or so years away. ONR aims to complete their GBAD by 2022 so it could find its way onto the new JLTVs soon. This will be a big change from the classic "Avenger" approach of Humvees with a .50-cal machine gun and Stinger missiles. The laser weapon should offer enhanced, effective lethality against ever advancing, proliferating drones and more.

LaWS – Lasers at Sea

Another forward leaning U.S. Navy laser program to arm ships is the Laser Weapon System, or LaWS. It is designed to target drones and light aircraft, but it could be useful in other scenarios, as well, such as small boat attacks trying to deny U.S. forces access to the shore.

Trials have been very successful so far. A 2011 test, for example, demonstrated that the weapon could destroy multiple small boats. A year later, this laser weapon downed several unmanned aircraft. Folks say this was the first ever takedown of a drone with a high energy laser mounted on a U.S. military vessel.

The LaWS system integrates six solid-state IR beams. Its design would allow the military to adjust how a threat is attacked. On the one end of the spectrum, it could issue a low output to cripple sensors or merely issue a warning; on the other end—it could let rip a high output to destroy a target.

The tech continues to advance and recent tests revealed that the pre-existing Phalanx Close-In Weapon System tracking system can handle tracking and targeting with the laser. Compatibility with Phalanx is great news. With Phalanx, there could be an effective range of 1.6 km and power from approximately 15 to 50 kilowatt.

RELI – 100 kW Solid State for Air, Land and Sea

Even more powerful lasers are underway for use by the military on land, at sea or in the air. The RELI project is set to develop a fieldable, high-power laser system that would be greater than 100 kilowatt and designed to fit a wide spectrum of military applications. The goal is directed energy that performs just as well moving as it does when it is stationary. At 100 kilowatts, this weapon is 10 times more power than the 10 kilowatt systems discussed earlier.

RELI's goals include improving high power electric lasers beyond the Joint High Power Solid State Laser. Another objective is to make them more militarized and fit for work downrange. RELI also seeks to increase system efficiency to more than 30 percent while generating excellent beam quality.

In 2010, companies began developing for the U.S. Army a 100 kilowatt-class weapons-grade laser system for defensive applications on land, sea and air platforms. The Army calls the program Robust Electric Laser Initiative, or RELI. The Army, the High Energy Laser Joint Technology Office and the Air Force are jointly participating in the RELI effort.

One of these companies was Boeing and three years later they announced that their Thin Disk Laser system surpassed the DoD's requirements for the RELI system. Thin Disk takes a series of commercial solid-state lasers and integrates them to produce one concentrated high-energy beam. This approach, leveraging commercially available lasers, provides a number of benefits like keeping costs down and ensuring they need minimal support and maintenance.

Boeing said blasts from its Thin Disk Laser surpassed 30 kilowatts in power, significantly surpassing DOD's initial goals and enough to do some serious damage to a battlefield threat. The demonstrations were the first time the system simultaneously achieved high power and high beam quality, which helps improve the laser's focus at longer ranges.

How does it work?

There are lots of different types of military lasers. The RELI program focuses on solid state ones—so called because they have a lasing medium that is solid crystal.

Lasing is the process that gets light particles excited enough to emit a particular wavelength. On their most basic level, lasers work by getting photons stimulated, concentrating them using something — in this case a solid like a prism — and then directing them into a beam.

Some of the biggest leaps in solid-state laser technology had been made through the U.S. military's Joint High Power Solid-State Laser (JHPSSL) program, which has ignited some major headway in this sort of tech.

Boeing has also been making progress in all sorts of military laser weapons. Notably, the company was awarded a U.S. Navy contract to develop the Free Electron Laser weapon system. The goal here is to build an ultra-precise laser gun to defend U.S. ships.

Northrop Grumman also began development to meet the RELI requirements. Northrop has a compact 25 kilowatt approach that combines laser beams into a single output beam for a field-ready laser weapon system. Their advances could result in a 100 kilowatt-class weapon system with good beam quality.

In 2014, Lockheed Martin announced they'd received a $25 million contract to design, build and test a 60-kilowatt electric laser. This laser would be integrated and tested in a truck-mounted weapon system demonstrator. The goal is to give warfighters a laser weapon that can defeat drones, mortars, artillery and rockets.

Under a contract managed by the U.S. Army Space and Missile Defense Command's Technical Center, the new ruggedized laser will be integrated on the High Energy Laser Mobile Demonstrator (HEL MD). This laser builds on the work the company has done under their Robust Electric Laser Initiative (RELI) contract for the Army.

HEL MD – Truck-Mounted 100 kW Laser

U.S. Army Space and Missile Defense Command/Army Forces Strategic Command has been developing the Army High Energy Laser Mobile Demonstrator (HEL-MD) program. A truck-mounted powerful weapon system like HEL MD could enhance tactical battlefield operations for the small unit at the brigade level.

Why is this important? Tragically, American warfighters are killed by indirect fire like mortars, artillery and rockets. Small drones are hard to see, hard to eliminate and ever proliferating. Lasers could be an ideal solution to all these sorts of all too frequent threats to U.S. personnel and aid workers.

Although 100 kilowatt is the military goal for HEL MD, several defense companies have been developing and demonstrating in field tests just how powerful, fast and precise lasers are at even 10 percent of that goal. Boeing is one of the companies developing HEL MD into a larger and more powerful directed energy, truck mounted weapon.

Throughout two test series, the Boeing HEL MD demonstrator successfully engaged more than 150 aerial targets such as incoming 60 mm mortars and drones. During these tests, HEL MD used a 10 kilowatt high energy laser installed on an Oshkosh tactical military vehicle. Back in 2014, this demonstrator was the first mobile, high-energy laser, counter rocket, artillery and mortar (C-RAM) built and demonstrated by the U.S. Army. Next steps could include installing a more powerful 50 or 60-kilowatt laser on HEL MD to demonstrate how it defeats threats.

With mortars, every split second counts. In tests, Boeing's HEL MD had a beam fixed on the threat within a few seconds—and the laser weapon successfully defeated more than 90 incoming mortar rounds and several drones.

How does it work?

HEL MD can be operated by a driver and an operator equipped with a laptop and an Xbox style controller. The laser is powered by lithium ion batteries that help to generate a highly focused, powerful beam of light. The batteries are charged by a 60 kilowatt diesel generator. How big does the laser beam need to be? In some of these tests, the beam was only about the size of a quarter, but still invisible to the naked eye.

To locate and designate targets, the system is designed with a telescope and infrared-based, wide field of view camera. The system tracks the moving target and aims the beam accordingly. Thus far, the system has performed extremely well in conditions that are very tough for lasers like wind, fog and rain.

Army test video revealed this laser system can target a mortar and cause it to burn up in mid-air. It is like taking a dangerous, explosive mortar and turning it into an inert chunk of rock as it hurtles through the air. Tests have also been very successful against large drones. And the laser has been so precise that the beam can be directed specifically at a tail to down the aircraft.

Once scaled up, it is expected that a 100-kilowatt version will be able to bring down a target at a speed ten times faster than the 10 kilowatt laser.

HELLADS – Aircraft Armed with 150 kW Lasers

DARPA aims to give the military an even more powerful laser weapon to fly the skies—and not in the distant future.

The High Energy Liquid Laser Area Defense System (HELLADS), has focused on developing a 150 kilowatt laser weapon system. The weapon will not just be a remarkable 150 kilowatt—the aim is to provide this immensely powerful weapon in a package ten times smaller and lighter than current lasers of that power.

Ultimately tactical aircraft, such as the Avenger Unmanned Aerial Combat Vehicle, could be armed. To achieve arming aircraft with this staggeringly powerful laser, it needed to be ultra light. HELLADS weighs less than five kilograms per kilowatt and is ultra compact at only three cubic meters big.

In 2015, HELLADS development had already reached enough laser power and beam quality for DARPA to start field tests against mortars, rockets, drones and mock surface-to-air missiles. The tests began at White Sands Missile Range, New Mexico.

In the same year, DARPA and the Air Force Research Laboratory began an effort to integrate the HELLADS laser into a ground-based laser weapons system demonstrator. After field testing, the plan was for the tech to transition to the military to further advance and refine for eventual operational use.

ABC – Fighter Jet Laser Turrets

Lasers on fighter aircraft? The Air Force is also looking for directed-energy pods—think laser cannon—that could be mounted on fighter jets within the next five years. The pods would be used to defeat enemy aircraft, drones, and missiles—but the goal is also to give the U.S. military a much lower cost per shot with them.

The system developed by Lockheed Martin is called Aero-adaptive Aero-optic Beam Control—ABC for short. The turret is in development for both DARPA and AFRL. The ABC turret system design means high-energy lasers can engage threats—whether enemy aircraft or missiles—above the aircraft, below the aircraft and behind the aircraft. Think 360 degree field of regard.

In 2014, Lockheed Martin announced that testing of laser turret for fighter aircraft was successful. With the 360-degree turret mounted on aircraft, the laser can fire in any direction. By 2015, more than 60 flights testing ABC proved successful and they'd managed to get the laser to work at jet cruise speeds—quite the feat.

Challenging

Why is it extremely difficult to get a laser weapon to work on a fighter jet? With a fighter jet, there is going to be atmospheric turbulence for starters and the challenge is developing a system that can crack this problem of atmospheric turbulence. Turbulence can scatter the light particles, making the laser ineffective. So how can it be counteracted? The laws of physics are against you. Those laws mean a laser can only engage a target in front of an aircraft that is travelling close to the speed of sound— that is unless a solution to atmospheric turbulence could be found.

To minimize this turbulence and deliver an effective beam, the ABC design harnesses new aerodynamic and flow-control tech. The optical compensation system together with mirrors help the beam penetrate the atmosphere and get on target. In the 2014 and 2015 tests, the flow control and optical compensation technologies successfully counteract the effects so it looks like laser cannons on military aircraft are indeed possible.

DE-STAR – Mega Powerful Lasers in Space

Could a sort of real-life version of a "Death Star" someday defend Earth against incoming threats from space?

Asteroid 2012 DA14 — about half a football field long and weighing about 130,000 metric tons — missed planet Earth back in a 2013 fly-by. Far smaller, and therefore harder to detect, was the roughly 65 foot long asteroid that injured more than 1,000 Russians when it stuck a few hours earlier.

What can we do about these dangerous asteroid threats? Some current options on the table include detonating a nuclear weapon near the surface. Detonating it below a threatening object in a sort of *Armageddon* way, or slamming a spacecraft into it to knock it off course.

The DE-STAR project believes developing a massive, orbital laser blaster that could someday defend against asteroid threats is possible—and a viable way to save the world. Two California scientists, Philip Lubin of the University of California Santa Barbara and Gary Hughes of California Polytechnic State University, conceived of a directed-energy orbital defense system could eliminate a threat on the scale of 2012 DA14 in an hour.

How does it work?

Designed to destroy or deflect an asteroid, DE-STAR— Directed Energy Solar Targeting of Asteroids—would harness the power from the sun and convert it into a massive phased laser beam array.

Basically, the laser beams would destroy or evaporate asteroids that pose a threat to Earth. It could also be used to deflect them away from the Earth or into the Sun. Simplified, the idea is that highly focused energy would raise the temperature on the target's surface in a particular spot to greater than 3000 K. The vaporization and release of surface material would then alter the orbit of the asteroid or comet threat.

And it even has the potential to destroy asteroids 10 times larger, the size of five football fields. It would take a year to vaporize an asteroid that gigantic, but it would start evaporating it from as far away as the sun. Theoretically, DE-STAR systems could also engage multiple targets simultaneously.

The DE-STAR system is apparently scalable, ranging from a desktop device to one as large as six miles long—the larger the system the greater its power. To put this into context, the DE-STAR 4 would be about 100 times the size of the International Space System could deliver 1.4 megatons of energy per day to its target. Their bigger version, the DE-STAR 6, could act as a massive orbiting power source and could propel a 10-ton spacecraft at near the speed of light making interstellar possible—according to their initial research.

When the project was announced, the scientists said it was based on current technology and enabled by advances in converting electrical power to light.

Lasers for space travel

If viable, the DE-STAR could also potentially be used for deep space exploration. The system could accelerate interplanetary travel speed and power deep space travel advanced ion drive systems. From an ambitious point of view, the tech could eventually evaporate an asteroid while simultaneously determine the composition of another...and throughout all these tasks also propel a spacecraft.

In 2015, the University of California's Santa Barbara's Experimental Cosmology Group received a grant from NASA to investigate the potential for directed energy as space travel propulsion. Photo-driven propulsion, the use of lasers as a means to power a spacecraft, could hold an important key to deep space exploration.

ELECTRONIC WARFARE

NEXT GENERATION JAMMER

To thwart adversaries attempting to target U.S. forces, jammers can make aircraft and troops "invisible" to enemy tech.

Preventing detection helps to enable effective strikes and also helps keep American fighters safe. But advanced jammers, and the jammers of the future, can also do much, much more. What's another amazing thing they can do? Jammers can even be used to create phantom aircraft to mislead enemy forces into believing other aircraft are in the air. Electronic warfare will play an increasingly massive role in future conflicts.

The U.S. military plans to dominate in this "e" terrain. Next Generation Jammers (NGJ), for example, will soon be joining the Navy.

NGJ is a cutting-edge electronic attack smart pod that will take the already-impressive Growler capabilities to an unprecedented level. Chosen to replace the legacy ALQ-99 systems used on the EA-18G Growler, one billion dollars of this electronic warfare tech will be amping up the fighter jet. In 2016, the U.S. Navy awarded a contract to Raytheon to build this Next Generation Jammer.

The NGJ will play a vital role in staying ahead of adversaries' capabilities. The tech will give the U.S. military even greater power, further enhanced precision, and a faster response time for electronic attack and electronic warfare counter-measures.

Growler

The NGJ will enhance one of the most advanced airborne electronic attack aircraft in the world: the EA-18G Growler. The Growler regularly provides tactical jamming and electronic protection to U.S. military forces and allies around the world.

A variant of the F/A-18F Super Hornet, the aircraft combines electronic attack with fighter aircraft speed and maneuverability. Typically crewed with one pilot and one weapon systems officer, Growler can reach speeds of approximately 1190 mph.

Ahead of ground, maritime, and other aircraft teams, Growler can enter the fight first, unleashing a devastating electronic attack. Using electronic attack tech, the aircraft can suppress enemy air and ground defenses.

By jamming enemy radar, Growler helps both air crews and ground strike teams to reach their target without being detected. In addition to jamming the adversary's communications over a broad frequency range, the ALQ-227 Communications Countermeasures Set also allows the Growler to locate, record, and play back enemy transmissions.

U.S. forces need to work in heavily jammed environments. The Growler brings to the fight its Interference Cancellation System to defeat these jamming systems and ensure uninterrupted radio communications for ground, maritime, and air forces.

Equipped with AIM-120 Advanced Medium-Range Air-to-Air Missiles, the Growler can also protect itself, as well as attack, enemy aircraft.

How does it work?

Electronic warfare capabilities are shrouded in secrecy and the NGJ is no exception.

In electronic warfare, radio waves, laser light or other directed energy are weaponized to disrupt, disable, or confuse the enemy's electronics. This type of capability also allows U.S. forces to sense incoming missile radar, listen to adversaries' radio signals, and more.

Very few details have emerged about the NGJ, but here's what can be shared. NGJ will involve a combination of agile, high-powered beam-jamming techniques together with truly next gen solid-state electronics. Many of the Growler's jamming capabilities fit in the gun bay and in two wingtip pods.

The military will receive fourteen Growler aeromechanical pods for airworthiness certification as well as fifteen Engineering Development Model pods for mission systems testing and qualification from Raytheon.

And this formidable electronic warfare capability is not in the far future. The Navy is aiming for operational capability in 2021.

FALCON SHIELD

By launching electronic attacks, Falcon Shield takes control of enemy drones and enslaves them to the will of the military. This system also provides the advantage that it hunts and locates drone threats—before enslaving them. Unveiled in 2015, Falcon Shield finds, fixes, tracks, identifies and defeats.

Mini-drones are becoming a growing security concern, as evidenced by the quadcopter drone mentioned earlier that crashed onto the White House grounds. Made by Finmeccanica-Selex ES, the Falcon Shield technology lets the good guys gain control of a drone whether a hobbyist accidental scenario or a deliberate terrorist one—and land them safely keeping folks out of harm's way.

The threat

Small-sized drones are cheap, widely commercially available, simple to assemble and easy to fly. These little drones can be hard to detect and stop. While it could be a child just having some fun, the concern is that the pilot could also be a terrorist or other adversary who has weaponized a small drone to act as a delivery method for threats like explosives or chemical and biological weapons.

The Falcon Shield is an adaptable system that can be deployed to protect VIPs. It could also be used to protect military convoys and patrols. Easily and rapidly portable, it doesn't need to be at a fixed location and teams can use it with flexibility where required. There are different versions of this Falcon Shield. For example, the variant carried by an individual will be different than the one for a vehicle. On a much larger scale, Falcon Shield can be used to protect a military base or a skyscraper that acts as headquarters for a big corporation.

How does it work?

The system monitors an assigned area to detect potential threats and protects a specified location by going through five stages of engagement.

Say a micro drone is targeting a VIP, for example, the good guys can fly it away from the target. They can force it to land at a safe location where a team can investigate and fully neutralize the threat.

In the first stage, Falcon Shield locates both the drone threat and the ground station controlling it. The tech then uses this data to guide the next stage. To "fix" the target, radar and electronic monitoring work together with an electro-optical infrared camera.

The camera and radar then track and identify the threat. In the final phase, Falcon Shield focuses on defeating the drone. When Falcon defeats a drone it doesn't just jam it- it seizes complete control of the drone.

How exactly the technology takes control of the drones is shrouded in secrecy... but take control, it does.

BIG AND LETHAL

PATRIOT

The United States and twelve more nations are set to get themselves even more powerful and reliable Patriots. The upgraded Patriot Integrated Air and Missile Defense system can destroy cruise missiles and aircraft with different kinds of interceptors.

The Raytheon-made system is prized for being able to identify incoming threats like enemy aircraft, drones, tactical ballistic and cruise missiles. When it locks onto a target, the system fires state of the art missiles to destroy the threat before it can cause any harm.

The Post-Deployment Build 8 (PDB-8) is an upgrade with a whole slew of enhancements to this iconic weapons system. The process is also about taking the lessons learned from the combat engagements of five nations and then combining that with knowledge gained from about 1,400 flight tests and more than 3,000 ground tests. The goal is to take all that together and apply it to creating further refinement and capability.

So what sort of advances will the military be leveraging in the future? In addition to improving the ability to destroy all types of threats, PDB-8 will also make the system better at detecting and identifying targets. The upgrades will enhance distinguishing between friendly and enemy aircraft. There will also be improved radar search capability. The Enhanced Weapons Control Computer is expected to bring 50 percent more computer power to help it better analyze and effectively address evolving threats.

User friendly

The enhancements are also focused on the end user. For the warfighters that use it, the PDB-8 aims to make operating it easier. Modern Man Station will give the user a color LCD display interface with touch screen and soft keys. Color symbology will help with friend or foe recognition and color will further enable rapid, and accurate, visual identification of threats. A ruggedized Radar Digital Processor will also be introduced. Combat proven Patriot is already highly reliable and it is expected that this new processor will increase this by a further 40 percent.

PAC-3 MSE

PDB-8 will allow the U.S. military to take advantage of PAC-3 MSE's advanced capabilities. PAC-3 MSEs destroy threats via the force of the collision. By contrast, GEM-T interceptors fly close to threats and then explode to destroy the missile or aircraft in the process.

In U.S. Army testing of the enhancements, they've successfully destroyed tactical ballistic missiles. During 2016 trials, the upgraded system successfully detected, tracked and engaged a cruise missile surrogate target. The PDB-8 followed with a GEM-T interceptor to destroy the target. The upgraded system then went against a tactical fighter aircraft target. It destroyed the aircraft with a PAC-3 MSE interceptor.

This latest 2016 test was a resounding success so the Patriot's PDB-8 upgrade is still on track for fielding in the very near future of 2018.

PHALANX CIWS

If a missile slips past a ship's defenses, then rapid-fire gun system Phalanx CIWS destroys the threat before it can strike—this is a "last-chance" defense system for military vessels. Made by Raytheon, Phalanx's 20 mm gun system automatically tracks and destroys enemy threats with computer-controlled radar. The weapon system is sometimes affectionately referred to as R2D2 because some folks think its iconic domed look, swiveling on its base, looks similar to the popular character.

The CIWS part stands for Close In Weapons System. And it's not just for missiles. Phalanx provides close-in defense against air, land and sea threats. It can take on a wide range of what an enemy throws at the ship from anti-ship missiles and low flying fixed-wing aircraft through to helicopters and fast-travelling surface craft. Phalanx can be used to detect, track and destroy threats that could manage to penetrate all other ship defense systems.

A Department of Defense contract at the end of 2015 meant that Phalanx will continue to be play a role at the top of its game. The contract provides for Phalanx CIWS to be made, maintained, inspected and tested—as well as four of the land version to be overhauled.

On land and at sea

The U.S. Army uses the land-based Phalanx as part of its systems to counter rockets, artillery and mortars. Before a threat can strike, Phalanx detects and destroys incoming rounds in the air. If there is an attack, the tech also provides early warning. The land-based version has also already been used in combat.

Rather than separate systems for searching, detecting, evaluating a threat—Phalanx does it all in one. It also handles tracking, engaging and destroying the threat.

Phalanx's Block 1B version features control stations that also allow its operators to visually track and identify threats before they are engaged. Additionally, there is a forward-looking infrared sensor.

Extending the defensive layer, the SeaRAM Anti-ship Missile Defense Systems uses the advanced Phalanx Block 1B sensors and replaces the gun with an 11-round Rolling Airframe Missile guide. The *Independence*-class of the U.S. Navy's Littoral Combat Ships carries SeaRAM.

The U.S. Navy announced it is acquiring about 160 million dollars more of Raytheon's Phalanx Close-In Weapons System (CIWS) in 2016. Phalanx is installed on U.S. Navy surface combatant ships as well as on the ships of many other countries.

EKV – Hit to Kill

At hypersonic speeds, the Raytheon-made warhead — a 120-pound spacecraft that has often been fondly described as a bunch of propane cylinders with a telescope mounted on it — operates at the edge of space to seek out and ram into threats...ultimately destroying them.

And get this—it doesn't rely on a single traditional warhead. It destroys serious threats by the sheer force of colliding with them at extreme speeds.

In 2013, the Missile Defense Agency quietly tested a "kill vehicle" at Vandenberg Air Force Base in California. The Agency successfully launched and tested the craft, which they call an Exoatmospheric Kill Vehicle or EKV. The Kill Vehicle successfully demonstrated that as the nation's first line of defense, it could block the threat of ICBMS—Intercontinental Ballistic Missiles.

EKV is an element of Boeing's Ground-based Midcourse Defense (GMD) system, which acts as the nation's shield. GMD is the first, and only operationally deployed system, to protect the homeland against intercontinental ballistic missile attacks. Currently, it is designed to counter rogue nation level capabilities like those of North Korea. Eventually, it will develop to defeat advanced ICBMs that more technologically adept countries may have. And this homeland shield is leveraging a hit to kill approach.

EKV destroys threats by using only the force of impact — this is a process known as "hit-to-kill."

Hit to Kill

GMD has sensors on land, sea and space to detect threats. Once a threat is detected, a three-stage solid rocket booster blasts the EKV into space. The EKV has its own propulsion, communications link, discrimination algorithms, guidance and control system. It also has its own computers and a rocket motor to steer in space.

Advanced multi-color sensors help to detect the incoming warheads.

So how does it hit to kill? The three-stage booster shoots this kill vehicle to a designated point in space. Once in space, the interceptor releases the EKV. It identifies the target, tracks the target and destroys the target—hitting to kill at hypersonic speeds. Again, the EKV does not carry a single traditional warhead and eliminates the target by force of impact alone at collision.

The 2013 test was the eighth in an extensive series ordered after the Flight Test Ground-Based Interceptor (FTG)-06 system failure in December 2010 — and a critical first step in returning GMD to successful intercept testing. A target missile launch was not included in this 2013 flight test, but the Missile Defense Agency said all components performed as designed. The program assessed and evaluated system performance in a flight environment using data gathered during this test.

In 2014, Raytheon's Exoatmospheric Kill Vehicle updated variant destroyed another intermediate range ballistic missile target in space. In this MDA event, the intercept took place during another test of Boeing's GMD. And since then, further tests have been underway as recently as 2016.

In addition to EKV, Raytheon is developing others in the kill family including Standard Missile-3 kinetic vehicle, Redesigned Kill Vehicle, and Multi-Object Kill Vehicle. The last time I checked in with the program, the Raytheon "Kill Vehicle" family had a combined record of more than 30 successful space intercepts.

EXALIBUR

More Exaliburs will be seen in battlefields of the future.

The Excalibur is a GPS-guided munition that allows warfighters to hit targets out of sight and miles away. Next gen cannon artillery, the U.S. military can use it to engage targets precisely at long ranges. Raytheon describes it as the longest-range, most precise, cannon-fired projectile in the world.

155mm Excalibur is currently a popular shell of choice downrange. It has certainly been very useful in combat. When close air support is unavailable, for example, Excaliburs can be very handy indeed. The shell uses jam-resistant GPS to maintain accuracy. Excalibur is known for accuracy, not just at long distances, but also in tight situations.

The Excalibur projectile is compatible with a range of systems including M777, M109s, M198, the Archer and PzH2000. It also works with G6, AS90 and K9 howitzers.

The first field test of an Excalibur round played out back in 2007 and it was in full rate production by mid 2014. The munition has continued to evolve and Raytheon has also been developing more variants.

To meet the U.S. Navy requirements, Raytheon is developing a five inch variant, the Excalibur N5. It uses the Excalibur Ib guidance and navigation unit. The goal is to provide more than three times the maximum range of conventional five-inch munitions while providing the same high level of accuracy of the land variant. In 2015 tests, at Yuma Proving Grounds, this new variant succeeded in direct hits on targets more than 20 nautical miles away.

The Excalibur S is another new variant that can redirect and adjust flight if the target moves. For GPS denied environments and GPS degraded areas, the newly added laser spot tracker will help compensate for errors—or GPS denied data—in target location error. It will also help with moving or relocated targets.

In 2016, the U.S. Army ordered 464 more Excaliburs Ib extended-range precision projectiles.

PERM

Precision Extended Range Munition — or PERM — will be joining Marines downrange.

In 2015, the United States Marine Corps announced this new, highly lethal round will support future combat operations.

The 120mm long-range, guided-mortar munition is smaller and will provide Marine expeditionary units with an Excalibur-like operational flexibility and precision lethality. PERM could increase first round effects while minimizing collateral damage. And it could mean fewer rounds are necessary to finish the mission.

What can it do?

Unlike Excalibur, PERM is tube-launched so warfighters can use it in confined spaces. And at 35 pounds, the shell is light enough to be handled by a single warfighter. It is hoped it could double the range of current 120 mm mortars to more than 10 miles.

PERM strikes distant targets that cannot be seen from the aiming position. Precision indirect fire like this will allow Marines to remain unseen or concealed from the enemy, while still effectively striking targets. And improved precision will also help to reduce risk to friendly forces, civilians and infrastructure.

In downrange conditions, wind and other factors mean that ballistic mortars require targeting adjustments. The farther the distance, the more these factors can change and the more impact these factors can have. It can make complete compensation extremely difficult, if not impossible.

PERM's system could make such tough calculations a thing of the past.

A robust versatile weapon system, it will work in all sorts of weather and all different types of terrain. It does not use rocket motors and instead uses tail fins for stabilization. For in flight adjustments, it has flaps near the nose.

The aim is to give Marines pinpoint accuracy to within ten meters of a target, but I've seen tests where the accuracy is as good as within a few meters. Depending on the target, PERM could also increase the lethality of the 120mm mortar by as much as 250 percent.

PERM represents an important advance to join the popular Excalibur because it could extend the current mortar capability range with enhanced accuracy. On a practical level in the field, this will mean critical targets like enemy artillery that may be currently beyond reach will become within striking distance with PERM.

ADVANCED PRECISION KILL WEAPON SYSTEM

This tech turns an ordinary unguided rocket...into highly advanced surgical strike.

Made by BAE Systems, the Advanced Precision Kill Weapon System takes standard unguided 70 millimeter rockets and transforms them into precision laser-guided rockets. To do so, it leverages semi-active laser guidance tech.

The APKWS technology fills the gaps between unguided rockets and Hellfire missiles. It is best suited for soft and lightly armored targets. And the key here is that it takes state of the art surgical strike and puts it in the hands of warfighters. It means readily available rockets can be quickly upgraded to precision weapons.

In future conflicts, urban terrains will continue to be a regular environment in which U.S. forces need to operate. Urban frequently means built up and confined areas where precision is paramount. Lack of precision risks collateral damage and civilian casualties. In these circumstances, U.S. forces could quickly upgrade rockets using APKWS. Thanks to the enhanced precision, teams can take advantage of opportunities to engage targets in confined areas where they would otherwise not have been able to strike before.

The tech is also designed to give aviators a highly accurate weapon that minimizes risk to non-combatants, forces and allies.

What does it take to upgrade rockets?

Rockets in the U.S. inventory can be easily converted without affecting the effectiveness of their fuses, motors and warheads. One advantage of this sort of plug and play technology, is that is allows the military to leverage the current inventories by simply upgrading as opposed to costly new acquisitions. The system does not require any modification to the aircraft or launcher—the only modification is to the rocket itself. Using standard tools, the guidance and control section can be inserted between the rocket motor and warhead.

Adapting it is simple—the unguided rocket is placed in a fixture and all it takes is a wrench to remove the fuse and warhead from the rocket motor. A guidance unit is then screwed into the rocket motor and the warhead and fuse screwed into the guidance section.

Before inserting the newly souped up rocket into the launcher, the pulse repetition frequency code matching the designating laser is dialed into it, the on/off switched placed on and the rocket is then ready to launch. And just that quickly, and easily, an unguided rocket is turned into a precision laser-guided one.

The modification can be made at the factory, a depot or even in the field. According to the company, minimal training is required to do so.

How does it work?

APKWS locks on after launch. Rocket fire can cause fire, debris and smoke damage so this timing means improved protection of guidance optics.

Within one second from launch, the battery engages the guidance section electronics, the wings are deployed and the trailing edges stabilize the rocket. Next the sensor aperture dome and seeker optics lock onto the laser painted target and guidance begins.

The low-cost laser guidance seeker aperture domes are mounted on leading edges of each wing. With innovative design and special seals, these seekers are protected from combat environment conditions such as sand, dust and debris.

The guidance system utilizes the same laser designator as the Hellfire. The system then determines the angle, pitch, roll and yaw controlled for precision flight to target.

Testing has demonstrated that APKWS sensors have acquired target data more than 14 kilometers away—a distance well beyond the range of its motor.

Aircraft

For the pilot, the laser targeting procedures and armament control are the same as current systems.

Any helicopter or fixed-wing aircraft capable of firing Hydra 70 rockets can use the Advanced Precision Kill Weapon System. BAE Systems is also looking to expand APKWS use to the MQ-8B Fire Scout and the armed MH-60S.

APKWS rockets can also be guided remotely by another aircraft, a targeting team on the ground or autonomously by using the aircraft's onboard system.

This new tech is not intended to replace high yield anti armor weapons like Hellfire missiles or for large area suppression. Instead it is best suited for precision engagement against moving and stationary targets. Its long-range laser acquisition and wide field of view would be handy against those sorts of targets.

The U.S. Navy and Marine Corps have been using APKWS since 2012. The U.S. Air Force began using the APKWS and fielded the tech initially for urgent F-16 and A-10 aircraft operational needs. In 2016, it was successfully used in combat operations. The U.S. Marine Corps fielded the APKWS on AV-8B fixed-wing aircraft and they have also been used by U.S. Army Apache helicopters in combat. APKWS is a smart, solution to be leveraged going forward in future combat.

HANDHELD

PIKE - Surgical Strike from Your Rifle

Pike is a powerful, precision-guided munition—that can be fired from a rifle-mounted grenade launcher. U.S. weaponeering is becoming so advanced that warfighters can now launch precision-guided munitions—by hand—and destroy enemy targets a mile and half away.

Precision guidance, an advantage associated with advanced missiles, increases lethality while reducing collateral damage. Raytheon has been taking the sort of powerful, and amazingly accurate, weapons that are typically seen on vehicles and aircraft and instead putting them literally into the hands of dismounted military teams.

Weighing in at a mere two pounds and just under a foot and a half long, the laser-guided Pike munitions punch well above their weight while providing that surgical strike advantage.

Raytheon markets the new tech as the world's only hand-launched precision-guided munitions. It is expected to give ground troops precision firepower at more than six times the range of some RPGs—and clearly with far greater precision.

What can fire a Pike?

Grenade launchers. And it can be fired from grenade launchers that are already regularly carried, like the single-shot 40 mm grenade-launching Heckler & Koch M320. Fired from a rifle-mounted grenade launcher, this 40mm caliber weapon is designed to hit a specific target and ensure minimal collateral damage. Its current accuracy is within five yards at a distance of a mile and a half.

How does Pike work?

A team of two warfighters working together can deploy Pike. One warfighter designates the enemy target, and the other fires.

Pike works best against targets that are stationary or slow moving and also at a mid-range distance. The first warfighter takes the laser designator device, which looks like a pistol, and points it at a target like an enemy-held building or vehicle. Then the second warfighter takes a rifle-mounted grenade launcher and fires the munitions. To engage, Pike uses a digital, semi-active laser seeker.

In addition to precision and distance, another key advantage for ground troops is that they would no longer need to use a vehicle launcher for this effect. Pike gives them the ability to fire off some hefty precision firepower while dismounted.

How is it different?

Like it says in the name, RPGs, or Rocket Propelled Grenades, use rockets. Pike is amped up with a rocket, too. But it features longer range with better accuracy. The

M32A1, popular with SOF for example, has a maximum firing range of about 400 meters at low velocity and you can get about 800 meters at medium. But its maximum effective range with a regular grenade is limited to about 375 meters.

On the other hand, in tests Pike has been delivering accuracy at about 2,300 — so that gives warfighters the power to destroy threats with precision at about 6 times further away than the M32A1 with a bog standard grenade.

Precision firepower at a greater distance means keeping U.S. warfighters safer. Generally, the farther away warfighters are while addressing a threat, the safer they are.

Because it uses a rocket engine, Pike accelerates more slowly than bullets or an artillery shell. The rocket motor ignites several feet after launch. Reportedly, when the rocket kicks in, Pike is nearly smokeless, which helps to reduce the launch signature, keeps the location of warfighters concealed, and helps to preserve an element of surprise too.

What's next? Raytheon is further developing Pike so that it can be fired from small boats and ATVs, like a Polaris Defense RAZR. It may also be able to fire from small drones.

SELF-GUIDED BULLETS – Sandia and EXACTO

Could new bullets make you into a world-class sniper?

Teams around the world have been working on just that...futuristic bullets that significantly enhance accuracy and range—as well as the ability to take on the toughest of moving targets. There are different approaches, but what they tend to have in common is that the bullets are "smart" and self-guided. Once the bullet leaves the rifle, it can modify its course and adjust to strike a target—even adjust dramatically to track a moving target.

In the U.S., Sandia National Laboratories and DARPA have proven most successful thus far at revolutionizing rifle accuracy and range with their homegrown first-ever guided bullets. The bullets are so remarkable that if they were ever made publicly available, then an American who enjoys hunting now and again could instantly deliver the marksmanship of a sniper. From a security perspective, bullets that could give anyone sniper abilities are not a good idea and make public release unlikely.

For the U.S. military, smart self-guided bullets could prove very useful.

SANDIA'S BULLET

Sandia's program has a fascinating story behind it.

Brian Kast and Red Jones, two hunters who also happen to work as engineers at the National Lab, developed this bullet initially in their spare time as a fun challenge—and built it with commercially available parts.

Unlike guided missiles in which corrections during flight can be slow, the Sandia bullet does not rely on an inertial measuring unit and corrections can be made an astonishing thirty times a second.

In 2012 tests, a 4-inch-long prototype from Sandia Labs demonstrated it could change direction in flight and hit a target more than a mile away, thanks to an optical sensor in its nose and fins for guidance. The sensor locates a laser trained on a distant target, while the bullet's brains process the data and steer the fins.

Not only did the battery and electronics work in their tests, the plastic sabots provided a gas seal in the cartridge — protecting the bullet's fins while it launched and successfully dropping off after leaving the barrel.

According to their patent, the self-guided bullet they built is accurate from half a mile away to within eight inches, while a normal bullet could be off by approximately thirty feet in "real world" conditions. Pitch and yaw are based on mass and size at a set rate. As the bullet flies down range it pitches less — and the accuracy actually improves the greater the distance to target.

In order to remove the spin that ordinarily allows rifle bullets to fly straight, Jones' and Kast's design puts the center of gravity forward and includes the fins that create aerodynamic stability.

Last I looked at this program, their self-guided bullet was not yet up to military speed and reached about Mach 2.1 (about 2,400 feet per second) using standard commercial gunpowder, but it was expected that a custom gunpowder might bring it up to military standard.

EXACTO

DARPA has been quietly conducting testing of its own self-guiding bullet system in the EXACTO Program— the Extreme Accuracy Tasked Ordnance. The ambitious initial aim was a guided .50 caliber bullet to introduce unprecedented accuracy at extremely long ranges, unhampered by crosswinds or target movements.

EXACTO is comprised of specially designed ammunition together with a real-time optical guidance system. The system helps track and direct projectiles to their targets. It does this by compensating for factors that can make successful hits tough such as wind, weather and target acceleration.

Military snipers with smart bullets

With an EXACTO small-caliber bullet that can continuously guide itself to a target, a military sniper with a standard rifle can hit moving and evading targets with even more extreme accuracy—and tests have proven snipers can do this at ranges unachievable with traditional rounds.

Like Sandia's approach, DARPA's bullet can change course during flight, using a real-time guidance system and control software that tracks and directs the bullet. And EXACTO is compatible with conventional sniper rifles.

Acquiring a moving target, such as an enemy in an accelerating vehicle, is already not easy. Add high crosswinds and the dusty terrain typical of places like Iraq and Afghanistan and you've got a real challenge. Yet speed and accuracy are crucial; any shot that fails to hit a target can potentially reveal presence and increase the risk to warfighter safety and the mission. This technology will let snipers engage moving targets at higher speeds, and at far greater range in tougher conditions than is currently possible.

Any Average Joe?

Progress with the self-steering bullet continues to be made. In 2015, the EXACTO program's live fire tests were very successful indeed. So successful...that an untrained, novice shooter managed to hit a moving target—on the very first time using the system.

And an experienced shooter was able to repeatedly hit moving and evading targets.

U.S. military sniper skills are remarkable and shooting at that level is in part an art, honed by unique talent and relentless practice. So the goal of EXACTO isn't to try to replace those unique skills, but instead to give snipers a self-steering bullet that can be used as a tool to help increase hit rates for difficult, long-distance shots.

EXACTO rounds have proven in testing that they can maneuver to not just hit moving targets—but to hit targets that are accelerating. And even targets that are evading.

If the DARPA tests—of both the DARPA bullet and optical sighting technology—continue on such a successful development trajectory, then the revolutionary tech will clearly give military snipers even greater range and enhanced accuracy. It is hoped EXACTO could reduce target engagement times by a remarkable fivefold.

Theoretically, a capability like this could help reduce risks to sniper teams by allowing them to take advantage of a wider range of covert positions.

And while EXACTO is being specifically tailored for snipers, it could also be applied to larger caliber guns. It holds great promise for air, ship and vehicle mounted systems. In order to miniaturize EXACTO's guidance capabilities into such a small .50-caliber size, lots of advances have had to be made. These advances could help unlock lots of potential for guided projectiles across all calibers.

SAGM – Smart Grenades

What if grenades could locate threats and detonate all on their own?

A new smart grenade can do just that. With this grenade, warfighters will know with certainty that it will strike its target. Smart Grenades could find enemies wherever they may try to hide. The U.S. Army has developed the SAGM, Small Arms Grenade Munitions round—and it seeks out bad guys.

With this new kind of grenade, whether an enemy hides behind an object, a wall or other would-be cover... it will defeat the threat. This is next-generation enhanced grenade lethality.

Why make grenades smart?

When enemies take positions behind—say, for example, the low mud walls typical of battle environments like Afghanistan—they can avoid grenade rounds. In order to most effectively hit a target, warfighters often require a direct line of sight with an M203 rifle-mounted grenade launcher and standard grenades.

A smart grenade could solve this problem. Just like other "smart" tech that can complete tasks without its user providing instructions, this smart grenade can find its target itself.

The SAGM is an air-bursting grenade and more than doubles the lethality of the current 40-mm grenade against targets that are not directly in a warfighter's line of sight.

When the SAGM is fired, the grenade will recognize its surroundings and the cover used by the enemy for concealment. It then detonates over the target. The idea is that even when an enemy is concealed, the SAGM will still be on target.

This 40 mm low-velocity grenade is compatible with the M203 and M320 rifle-mounted grenade launchers used by the Army.

How does it work?

Using an SAGM, a warfighter would not need to do any sort of pre-fire programming sequence. The warfighter just needs to accurately aim the weapon and fire — the smart grenade will take care of the rest. While in the air the SAGM will detect walls, without even relying on a range finder. After it passes the wall, the SAGM explodes itself in the air above the target.

To be truly versatile and effective downrange, the SAGM will need to be able to detect and process a wide range of objects that adversaries may hide behind. The Army is working on developing a sensor system that will make the SAGM so smart it can do just that.

They've made the fuze "smart" by including sensors. The sensors and logic devices scan and filter the environment, detect the obstacle, figure out the best place to detonate and then autonomously airburst the fuze.

The grenade is designed to have three firing modes. The first one is the airburst after it detects the cover where someone is concealed. The next is a default detonation when it hits the target called "point detonation." The third mode is a self-destruct feature. This final one is designed to decrease collateral damage and reduce unexploded ordnance left on the battlefield.

The Army had also been developing the XM25 grenade launcher as a direct fire method for these sorts of concealed targets. This weapon uses an on-board laser system to gauge distance to its target. It has a programmable airburst round that determines the distance to its target. The SAGM, on the other hand, is designed for indirect fire.

What's next?

A team at the U.S. Army's Armament Research, Development and Engineering Center at Picatinny Arsenal in New Jersey began developing the SAGM and undertook substantial testing in 2015. The program continues to refine and advance. ARDEC's mission is to develop technology and engineering solutions for America's warfighters.

AMPED UP AT4S

The shoulder launched AT4 is one of the most popular weapons in the world and it has been amped up even more. With the new souped-up AT4, users can defeat more types of enemy targets, in more challenging conditions and at further distances.

The robust and reliable AT4 is lightweight, disposable, and easily shoulder-launched. To provide an even higher hit-probability, this variant has a refined launch system. And its singular warhead design ensures a very high kill probability.

Warfighters need to focus on the threat at hand and shouldn't have to waste time and thought on manipulating a weapon.

The AT4 perfectly fits this need. It is extremely easy to operate and handle, if you are facing a threat, you simply take aim and fire. The target is destroyed and you can discard the empty tube. It is so easy to use that you don't need to be an expert, or even have much training, to operate the weapon with great success.

Building on the modularity of the 84 mm caliber system, the new addition to the AT4 weapons family delivers extended range and improved high explosive effects. In fact, all the enhanced variants deliver extended range performance and improved high explosive effects. The idea is that they give warfighters more flexibility, in more scenarios to defeat threats.

All AT4 weapons, including this latest addition to the family, are single-shot and fully disposable. Designed to withstand combat conditions, the 84 mm caliber disposable weapon weighs just over 15 pounds, and is about three feet long.

Instead of a clip on sight, the AT4m features a red dot sight that is integrated into the weapon. This further increases the ease in using the weapon since it's the same sight for training and all light conditions in combat.

Options

The AT4 family is a range of lightweight, man-portable, fully disposable weapons. For each fired weapon, the result is a very high target kill probability.

When warfighters are dismounted from vehicles, they leave the safety of that armored protection. If they come across an enemy-fighting vehicle, then they need some serious firepower to defend themselves. Armed with AT4 Anti-Armor, then they can defeat these threats. It gives troops a high muzzle velocity and high armor penetration.

The AT4 HEAT can penetrate enemy armor more than 420 mm. This AT4 is effective against armored vehicles and structures and has a range from about 130 feet to over 1,300 feet. It's also disposable when it has been fired.

If warfighters need to raid a structure, then they may want to make their own entrance. Doors and windows in target structures can often be booby-trapped and dangerous. The AT4 CS AST is the right choice for this objective. It has zero recoil and is great at close combat range. If the goal is to destroy a structure, then by simply adjusting the setting, this AT4 can take out that stronghold.

The AT4CS HE allows warfighters to engage enemy troops in airburst or impact mode out to a distance of approximately 330 feet. The AT4CS ER takes the anti-armor capability of the AT4 Confined Space and extends its effective range to nearly 2000 feet.

MORE M4

Fan of the M4A1 and M4? So is the U.S. Army. More of the popular weapons will be making their way into the hands of troops. In 2015, the Army ordered $212 million more M4 and M4A1 carbines from Colt Defense and FN America.

M4

A classic, the M4 combines lightweight mobility with effective firepower. The 5.56-mm carbine was designed to meet the U.S. military's high performance standards.

It's got a fourteen and a half-inch barrel and with the stock extended the weapon is 33 inches long. The rate of fire is 700 to 950 RPM and the M4 has an effective range of about 600 meters, or 1,969 feet.

In 2013, the military had also placed a $77 million order with FN for 120,000 more M4s. Attempts to replace the popular M4 with another weapon have not been successful. Instead, the weapon has been improved through programs like M4s to M4A1s and the M4A1+ initiative.

M4A1

The M4A1 has been popular with SOF for about two decades.

The Army began modifying nearly half a million M4s to upgrade them to M4A1s. And these M4A1 carbine rifles have been rolling out in stages to warfighters. The Army is expected to finish the conversion of M4s to M4A1s by 2020.

The conversions mean that the M4A1s weigh a bit more, but once modified they can offer a lot of advantages, such as in suppressing fire. The barrel is heavier by a few ounces, but it provides better resistance to heat and it enables shooting longer strings of fire with accuracy.

The conversion also includes a shift from three-round burst to fully automatic. And good news for lefties, this version provides ambidextrous safety controls.

M4A1+

The M4A1+ program aims to further enhance the weapon.

The "plus" in M4A1 includes changes like an extended 12-inch forward Picatinny rail. This lets warfighters attach more accessories like laser sights, optics, lights and pointers to capitalize on the benefits they provide. The front and rear iron sights will be removable.

M4A1+ is meant to have better accuracy—no farther than five inches from the target at 300 meters throughout the life of the barrel. The shift to a floating barrel will help to improve accuracy. An advanced flash suppressor reduces firing signatures during both night and day missions. The "plus" also provides an optional sniper-style single-stage trigger.

The contract to supply the new M4s and M4A1s runs through 2020. The Army also recently ordered $84 million worth of M240 machine guns from FN America.

LAND

ARMORED VEHICLES

ADAPTIV – Invisibility Cloak + Chameleon Armor

Invisible tanks seem far-fetched? Not anymore. At least not in the battlespace where adversaries often rely on "seeing" in infrared.

Not only can new tech called ADAPTIV make tanks "invisible," it can provide chameleon-style capabilities. A tank protected with this tech could convince the enemy they were seeing say, a cow, instead of an armored vehicle.

Adaptiv — an armor encasing that looks and feels as one imagines a dragon's scales to — turns tanks into chameleons, allowing them to disappear into the environment behind them or to even look like a snow drift, trash can, crowd, or a soccer mom's station wagon. A product of BAE working alongside the Swedish Defence Material Administration, Adaptiv rocks absolutely cutting-edge camouflage technology.

BAE Systems unveiled this futuristic tech at one of the largest weapons shows on Earth, the biennial Defense and Security Equipment International (DSEI) held in London, England. In 2011, this new "Chameleon Tank" quickly became the star of the show and made international headlines. Since then the tech has continued to quietly advance at a phenomenal rate. This BAE team, comprised of some serious defense tech innovation All Stars, continues to relentlessly push the envelope making the stuff of science fiction a reality. As you'd expect for a technology this groundbreaking and coveted, the security surrounding the tank was both immense and intense.

The team gave me one of the first looks during the Big Reveal. To evaluate just what Adaptiv could bring to combat, I invested a fair bit of time to truly put it through its paces. Folks quickly dubbed it a real life "invisibility cloak." So what was in like in person? The scales were cool to the touch in spite of the incredible work they were undertaking. Every time I put on optics, I saw firsthand that big, heavy tank completely vanish. Every subsequent test, the tech was so effective that I found myself just as astonished as the very first time. It never became less remarkable that they achieved making a large tank completely vanish before my "eyes."

Arguably even more amazing in person is the chameleon factor. I also gave the chameleon capabilities a very, very thorough tire kicking so to speak. I challenged the team—and the truly cutting-edge tech—with a very wide range of ordinary daily objects. I chose objects that you might see downrange and ones that you might see on a typical London street. Each challenge was met effortlessly and rapidly. Before my eyes, one moment it would look like a tank and then in the next it would become a "dog" wandering around a "trash can."

In a war zone and need your tank to look like a herd of goats? No problem. Instant transformation. Truly extraordinary stuff.

Eyes in the battlespace

The key to remember here is that Adaptiv, at this time, could only pull off these feats if you were looking at it through devices that "see" in infrared. In a very simplified way, here is how that works. The human naked eyes sees the visible light spectrum, but next to it there is an infrared spectrum. There are three categories: near IR, mid IR and thermal IR. With near and mid infrared, it is about reflection off objects. With thermal, the object emits the heat.

Anything that uses energy, whether it's a human or a tactical vehicle, gives off heat. Atoms fire off photons in the thermal-infrared spectrum because of the heat. Night vision devices can harness thermal imaging to "see" these infrared emissions and reveal someone, or something, that is attempting to be concealed.

In Sweden, research began at the end of the nineties to look at the proliferation of sensors on the battlefield and to consider how they could meet this threat and defeat the advantage those sensors could give the enemy. The team looked at the best thermals to date and reverse engineered them focusing on 500 meters.

Infrared, used by devices such as night-vision goggles or aircraft, essentially sees in hot and cold, unlike the human eye. Adaptiv uses the reliance on thermals in the battlespace against adversaries by manipulating these hot and cold readings to deceive the enemy who is scanning for forces.

Adaptiv research is very highly protected with good reason, but what I can say is that the tech has continued to evolve and is even more capable than at the time of the public unveiling.

Invisibility with dragon-like scales

A system of more than 1,000 5.5-inch hexagonal tiles made of thermo-electric material gives the tank its "invisibility cloak" and chameleon-like abilities. The scales can help confuse (if not convince) an adversary into thinking he is looking at something he is not. Hesitation can give the warfighters a few more seconds— and in some scenarios even a split second can make all the difference on the battlefield.

How does it work? The tiles or pixels can rapidly change temperature. Thermal cameras monitoring external temperature direct them to do so. By quickly projecting adjustments onto them, the Adaptiv tank can match the temp of the immediate environment and blend into it...vanishing.

In this blending mode, it matches the temperature of its surroundings, melding with the background to avoid detection. Blending can even be achieved when the tank is moving, and the initial trials suggested that blending was at its best at 300 to 400 meters.

Sure Adaptiv's got this invisibility power, but arguably even more remarkable is its ability to shapeshift to the eyes of infrared. Disguising vehicles as tanks with paint or netting is nothing new, but Adaptiv does it in a far smarter and futuristic way.

Chameleon

How does the tank appear as a soccer ball in the eyes of an enemy? To transform into an entirely different object, Adaptiv draws from its pattern library organized by terrain. It projects itself as something native to the immediate area. For example, if it enters an Arctic environment it can conjure up a polar bear and project itself as one. Sensors scanning for a tank would then "see" a native animal—not an adversary.

Adaptiv is not limited by its pattern library however, and can even go chameleon on the fly shifting into something it has come across in its immediate terrain. As just one example, if it is entering an urban environment Adaptiv can take a snapshot of an object on the local street like a mailbox and then immediately change its appearance to be read as a mailbox to scanners.

Mounted on the tank is a large-ish ball with an array of cameras; press a button to capture an image and another to push that image out to the scales of the tank to go chameleon. It is that simple.

The armor also serves another very important purpose. Friendly fire is always a concern, and demarcating to your force as a friendly, and not hostile, is key. This signal needs to be discreet as well, so that you are not advertising to the enemy.

Planes, for example, sometimes use a method of radiating their identity in all directions; Adaptiv is also capable of signaling its identity to only the friendly side in a cunning way. By projecting onto its skin a marker similar to a barcode, it can indicate it is a friendly in a way that is only readable to its force. The team proved to me how effective it was by emblazoning my name on the side of the tank – but only visible to those who held the key.

Armor

Balancing weight with protection is always a challenge. Heavy armor may seem to make warfighters safer, but the additional weight can slow a vehicle down and reduce its agility — thereby increasing possible risk.

In addition to invisibility and chameleon solutions to protection, the Adaptiv armor provides traditional armor protection. It can withstand ordnance and physical impact, consumes low power and is relatively lightweight so it does not affect agility or movement.

What if the Adaptiv-protected vehicle takes a hit? Downrange if a pixel is damaged, it can easily be removed and replaced.

The pixels can be scaled up or down so there are a bunch of other applications as well. Taking a helo on a search and rescue mission as an example, the pilot could wield Adaptiv armor to make the helicopter appear instead to the enemy like a cloud – helping keep the mission covert and safe.

Warships kitted out with Adaptiv could theoretically enjoy the advantage of looking like a wave—not a warship—to bad guys. The tech could also be applied to structures, like a forward operating base, to make them "invisible" or appear like a pile of rubble.

The pixels can be resized to achieve stealth at different ranges. For example, larger objects like buildings or warships might not require close-up stealth and may be fitted with larger panels to display a lower resolution image.

Adaptiv could be a game changer. There are clearly lots of advantages to deploying tanks, and really anything else, that appears "invisible." But one advantage that particularly resonates with me is force protection. It is hard to kill something that you can't see or find.

What's next?

What's next for Adaptiv? I hear they are playing with other light frequencies such that invisibility to the naked eye could someday be a possibility—and as for the other mind-blowing advances in the pipeline for this...unfortunately they can't be shared with the public, but may be hitting a battlespace in the not so distant future.

BATTLEVIEW 360 – See Through Tanks

What if tank crews could see through the heavily armored walls of their vehicle? New tech, also made by the folks at BAE Systems, can make tank armor seem transparent to the crew and friendly forces.

This new, cutting-edge tech is called BattleView 360. By wearing the helmet-mounted tech, a crew member can "see through" the tank out to the surrounding battlefield —and other members of the force, whether back in the U.S. or in another nearby vehicle, can "see" what the tank crew's "eyes" see too.

Innovation has long been underway to give fighter pilots this sort of capability. The F-35 helmet, covered in the *Air* section of this book, utilizes cameras and sensors fixed around the outside of the aircraft to provide pilots with a 360-degree view. In a sense, the helmet let's fighter pilots "see through" the floor of the aircraft, down to the ground. The concept with the armored vehicles is the same—but on the ground. With BattleView 360, tank crews and commanders will have a complete view of the battlespace around them in real time—no matter how heavily armored the vehicle is.

The heart of BattleView is a digital mapping system. It collates, tracks and displays the position of anything of interest to a tank crew in the surrounding area. And it can do this in two-dimensions, or in three.

Why use it?

BattleView 360 could provide a number of key benefits and one that could not be overstated is taking the element of surprise away from the enemy. From inside heavily armored vehicles, it can be tough for crews to know what is going on outside. Personnel have to contend with both the noise and the limited visibility typical of highly armored vehicles.

Since seeing outside the vehicle can be tough, egress can be a particularly dangerous moment. Enemies could be lurking outside for an ambush, but unseen to the crew members before they dismount.

By wearing a BattleView enhanced helmet, crews gain 360-degree situational awareness. Warning messages— like that an enemy is approaching— as well as critical mission updates are relayed directly to the helmet. BattleView is also designed to give crews the advantage of quickly engaging more targets and more rapidly confirming to shoot.

For the tank driver, the tech gives him "external eyes." The driver can also choose to overlay the external 360-vision with other useful data like terrain input and additional symbols to aid navigation.

How does it work?

There are two ways warfighters can interface with BattleView 360- through headgear and a rugged tablet. A crew member can opt for the special high-tech lens that mounts on the helmet. The way the headgear works is a translucent lens sits in front of one eye, kind of like Google Glass. Data is projected onto it, and the warfighter can "see through" the tank with that eye.

A touchscreen can also access the system and display the 360 view.

Both sync to cameras and sensors mounted outside the vehicle. It is this syncing that provides the real time ability for crews to "see through" the heavily armored walls. The sensors collect the data used to build a 360-degree view of their surroundings. The cameras can feed both visual and infrared light—giving the warfighter the option to quickly choose to see in either way.

Warfighters equipped with the tech can then further enhance their view of the battlespace with overlaid information and symbology. Information and visuals can also be provided beyond the sensors on the tank itself.

While BattleView 360 harvests data from sensors and cameras on the tank or other armored vehicles, it can also let the warfighter see through a range of "eyes," and overlay data immediately from other sources too. Dismounted warfighters, for example, can use BattleView to send information back to the vehicle.

Eyes Everywhere

Using the naked eye while inside a heavily armored tank, there's an extremely limited range of view. This tech gives crews a sort of "pick and mix" of eyes to choose to see through. BattleView 360 means crews can receive all sorts of vital data from the feeds. While still inside a tank, crews can gain a bird's eye view of the battlespace by opting to "see" through the eyes of a drone above. Or crews can choose to "see" through the armor of other armored vehicles to "see" exactly what they are "seeing" from inside their tank. Whether a robot is tackling an IED, or travelling through the battlespace to provide reconnaissance or surveillance, crews can even opt to "see" through the "eyes" of ground robots.

Evasion

The tech provides an amazing range of eyes in real time and that is impressive. But the state of the art tech also goes beyond that. The system is smart and harvests what it "learns" from all the "eyes" it can see through and processes it. Why? It analyzes the data to help advise warfighters.

It can do tank route planning, monitor progress and flag friendly forces. But it can also do other critical calculations by itself, like determine the best route to avoid enemy detection.

That's right, BattleView 360 can also help devise ways to evade the enemy. How does it work? There is a red ground display that demarcates the ground that hostile forces can see—making it clear what route not to take. The technology can flag areas of uncertainty from last hostile sighting, and figure out the most likely routes an enemy would take.

Commanders

The tablet style display provides certain advantages to a commander.

BattleView overlays crucial data that help commanders gain a full picture of the battlefield. As just one example, the system gathers, collates and displays data on friendly and enemy forces to help a commander rapidly identify and distinguish them. The gathered data and enhanced "vision" supports a commander figuring out safer routes.

In addition to aiding in quick, well-informed decisions, the BattleView tech also lets a commander communicate crucial data, like plans, directly to other tanks, vehicles, dismounted forces, and HQ. The enhanced 360-picture of the battlefield could also be leveraged for targeting decisions. Tank commanders can even view a gunner's, or any other crew member's, display on his screen at any given time.

BattleView 360 can be integrated into both existing and new vehicles, and could be introduced to give warfighters this ultra-enhanced vision and situational awareness in future fights.

AJAX

In future combat, armored fighting vehicles will be smarter, faster and more maneuverable without compromising force protection.

In Greek mythology, Ajax was a formidable warrior characterized by his colossal size, strength and honor. He served in the Trojan War. A warrior in Homer's 'Iliad,' one of Ajax's hallmarks was a powerful shield.

To meet the demands of militaries fighting in the future, General Dynamics created AJAX—an armored fighting vehicle that will bring greater firepower, protection and maneuverability to future fighting forces. And like its namesake, AJAX the armored fighting vehicle of the future will provide a powerful shield to forces.

The turreted AJAX heavily armored Scout Specialist Vehicle prototype was unveiled by General Dynamics in 2015 and is set to replace the FV107 Scimitar. The Alvis-made Scimitar entered service in 1971. Fun fact: Lore has it that Jaguar, perhaps more commonly associated with luxury vehicles rather than fighting ones, gave the Scimitar its engine.

If you're going to name a vehicle after a colossal war legend, then it had better bring a lot more to future fights—and the AJAX does indeed.

Reveal

When the prototype was unveiled, I had the chance to literally climb all over it to properly get to grips with every detail. My professional curiosity would have lead me to be thorough anyhow; but it was further fortified by the fact one of my very good British Army officer friends and his regiment would be AJAXed soon so he'd made me promise to report back. Sometimes the heels have to come off and a good clamber undertaken to truly get a proper, close look.

So what did I find? AJAX will certainly bring more armor, more sensors, more firepower and more maneuverability. The vehicle also has a two-person turret that was developed by Lockheed Martin, and it can carry a crew of four. It is designed to provide ISTAR (Intelligence,

Surveillance, Target Acquisition and Recognition) and to yield maximum reconnaissance data. This new Scout Specialist Vehicle brings a stabilized 40mm Case Telescoped Cannon and a 7.62mm coaxial machine gun to the fight.

AJAX is part of a family of next-gen armored fighting tracked vehicles. Its siblings all have names like Athena, Ares, Apollo, Argus and Atlas drawn from Greek mythology too. In addition to a turreted version, there will be five other non-turreted Ajax variants. Each will feature different armor, designed for specific roles in the battlespace. To name just a few other examples, you can expect an armored repair and tow vehicle as well as an engineering recon vehicle equipped with a plow to join the family.

Each variant features tailored capabilities such as a laser warning system, acoustic detectors and an electronic countermeasure system. Other enhancements focus on different handy things like a route marking system and a local situational awareness system.

General Dynamics will be building 589 AJAX vehicles for the British Army. Of these, 245 will be the turreted model.

When will we see the future armored fighting vehicle AJAX in combat? The first ones are set to arrive in 2017 with all 589 due to be delivered and ready to join the fight by 2024.

DARPA GVX-T

What if you could create an armored fighting vehicle that combines all the speed, agility and off-roading of a next-gen ATV with protection that is even better than a tank's?

DARPA regularly makes the impossible, possible. And the Agency is committed to giving the U.S. military the best armored fighting vehicle of the future. The DARPA project team leader is a force to be reckoned with. While discussing the project recently, he was able to throw out some ingenious solutions off the cuff that I'd never heard even once before—and keep in mind I hear a whole lot of would-be solutions to future combat challenges on a daily basis from the most talented minds. Even water cooler talk in my world usually centers around future combat and future threats. Under his leadership, I'm certain that this vehicle will have features that even the most imaginative Hollywood films have yet to portray or consider.

Dubbed the GXV-T for now— which stands for Ground X-Vehicle Technology— this fighting vehicle will be full of groundbreaking DARPA tech for the U.S. military, tech that will make it more agile, fast, safe and affordable than current options.

And this new vehicle worthy of Jason Bourne's most ambitious missions could be in the hands of the U.S. Army and Marine Corps someday soon. DARPA has chosen eight companies to try to create everything on their wish list and to devise a fighting armored vehicle that will eclipse all others in the battlespace.

Aside from producing an outstanding ride—why it is important? Weapons continue to evolve and become more and more effective at piercing through the armor that protects military ground vehicles. The current solution tends to be to add more armor. This can provide more protection—but it also tends to translate into more weight and less speed, agility and maneuverability.

Shifting Armor

More armor is old school. DARPA has challenged companies to find a solution that does not involve additional armor, and thus more weight. Instead companies must innovate and figure out how to completely rethink conventional approaches to armoring.

One solution could be a sort of shape-shifting armor that automatically repositions itself to fortify against, and defeat, an incoming threat. How would that work in practice? Consider this scenario: you're on a mission and you've pulled over and parked to have a good old fashioned look at a paper map or maybe to take a nap. The bad guys spot you, the now stationary target, and try to lob off a grenade. You take as much notice of this as you would a feather floating by your window because all by itself the vehicle has long since spotted enemy movement, noted the incoming threat and already reconfigured the armor directing it to exactly where the grenade will strike. The impact is absorbed as if it never happened—so you can carry on your snooze undisturbed.

This is, of course, an ideal world scenario...even if the companies can crack automatic reconfiguration that would be a much needed leap ahead.

Hitching a flight into the fight

DARPA created a video to showcase some of the features the GXV-T could bring to the fight. The vehicles are seen flying through the air, having hitched a ride with a helicopter. Designed to be lightweight and readily transportable, the vehicles are then dropped and inserted into the battlespace.

ALLISON BARRIE

Once on the ground, the GXV-T would dominate off-road. This puppy won't just be able to go off-road— it will be able to effortlessly handle 95% of the world's terrain. DARPA has challenged companies to devise advanced suspension and novel track and wheel configurations to make this possible.

It will also bring extreme speed to the fight. Break-throughs are expected to ensure that this speed is truly extreme—both on and off the road—and better than what is possible with current vehicles.

A vehicle that "thinks" and adapts

Let the team focus on the mission, while the vehicle takes care of the rest. When their eyes are not on the road, this GXV-T will automatically avoid obstacles.

DARPA aims to provide the U.S. military with lots of breakthroughs with advanced tech on the "crew augmentation" front too.

One idea is to take modern commercial airplane cockpits and give the best of their self-automation style capabilities to a ground vehicle. So while a squad focuses on the mission or returning fire against a threat, the vehicle could handle the driving for them.

It will also provide futuristic degree of data. GXV-T gathers and displays everything they need to know about the nearby enemy. GXV-T even automatically avoids enemy detection. How can it do this? The vehicle could be so smart that it anticipates and predicts enemy move-ments, rapidly figures out alternative routes to avoid engaging them and then takes those routes while driving itself.

Stealth

With the proliferation of advanced tech around the world, staying stealthy is becoming increasingly difficult. But DARPA aims to ensure that teams driving the GXV-T can evade detection with state of the art "signature management" tech. Signature management is basically a fancy way of saying don't get caught, spot threats and targets first without being seen yourself.

GXV-T will stay stealthy by reducing signatures that would traditionally be used to detect it. At the same time, it would reveal those attempting to be stealthy. This vehicle will not be detectable by infrared, sound, sight, and electromagnetic.

But the vehicle won't just be stealthy, it will be smart stealthy. It will be able to spot enemy forces and threats before it can be seen itself—and notify the human team onboard.

In the video, DARPA shows some possible scenarios. The smart vehicle alerts the team that it has made visual contact with opposing forces and on futuristic displays provides data and instructions to detour to a secondary valley route, successfully avoiding engagement with the enemy.

So the vehicle itself will be able to identify threats and immediately "think" of ways to avoid detection. It could then advise the team accordingly. And as in the example earlier, it may even be able to just avoid detection automatically—sort of an enemy evasion autopilot.

To have these stealthy smarts, advances in tech will need to be made like high-resolution sensors that can help build 360-degree high-resolution images of the world outside the vehicle and the battlespace.

Eight companies, seven hailing from around the United States and one UK-based, are in contention to be selected to develop this futuristic ride. The teams that have been chosen are: Carnegie Mellon University, Honeywell International Inc., Leidos, Pratt & Miller, Raytheon BBN, Southwest Research Institute, SRI International and QinetiQ Inc. DARPA has awarded a contract to each.

TERRAMAX – Optimus Priming Trucks

While not yet at Optimus Prime level, Oshkosh Defense has made serious headway on a robotic truck that "thinks" and can "lead." This new tech means a truck can drive itself to a forward operating base through a dangerous area to deliver much needed resupply. It can even lead, or be part of a robot truck convoy, transporting large amounts of supplies to remote regions—without a single human in the convoy.

Known as TerraMax, the tech can make vehicles "smart" and able to work on their own. TerraMax is frequently demonstrated enhancing the Oshkosh's Medium Tactical Vehicle Replacement (MTVR) defense truck platform.

These futuristic TerraMaxed trucks can be taught a mission and work together as a convoy to reach a destination by themselves, reacting and adapting along the way to complete the mission. They're smart enough to detect and avoid obstacles along the way. They're even smart enough to detect and avoid the enemy.

There are different degrees to human involvement. TerraMax can have humans onboard and behind the wheel. A warfighter can also program TerraMax to autonomously follow a route or a lead truck. If the lead vehicle in a convoy is attacked, it's easy for the operator to reprogram the truck to follow a new leader.

Or TerraMaxes can conduct missions in a war zone while directed by a human operator sitting anywhere in the world.

Why make a robotic truck?

Logistic convoys are frequently attacked and under IED threat, so it's critical to get warfighters out of the cabs of vehicles if possible.

How does it work?

Equipped with a military grade Global Navigation Satellite System (GNSS), TerraMax uses radar to avoid obstacles and very high definition LIDAR—Light Detection and Ranging— to understand ground surfaces. Correctly interpreting standing water is always a big challenge, but when I saw TerraMax in action it seemed like they've even made excellent progress on that front.

For such advanced tech, tele-operation is very straight forward. Familiar with game consoles? Then you could get to grips with directing TerraMax pretty easily. This smart truck can be driven by an Xbox-like console. The interface with the "robot" is designed to be easy and intuitive for operators. A single operator can oversee several trucks with just a ruggedized touch-screen tablet and the video game-style handheld controller.

For a warfighter operating it, managing the robotic convoy it is also very similar to using a Blue Force Tracker. From the console, you can even set tire inflation, lock configuration, adjust thresholds and range of deviation in obstacle avoidance.

Using a combination of GPS, radar, LIDAR and multispectral cameras with overlapping redundancies, the technology allows the truck to either navigate itself from point to point, with the ability to avoid unexpected obstacles along the way. Or it could deploy to clear IEDs and be controlled remotely by an operator at a safe distance.

Why are trucks that can conduct missions by themselves important?

Traveling on, and clearing, IED infested roads are two very dangerous tasks that the U.S. military will continue to face. Tragically, thousands of American warfighters have been injured and killed by IEDs in U.S combat operations in Afghanistan and Iraq. In future conflicts, IEDS are expected to persist as a serious threat.

If smart trucks could be achieved, then robots could tackle the transport jobs on dangerous roads where IEDs can lurk—and reduce the risk to U.S. personnel by doing so.

And what if smart trucks could go a step farther and actually clear mines to make roads safe for troops?

That's exactly what Oshkosh Defense is proposing with this unmanned military machine. The idea is that an TerraMaxed M-ATV fitted with a mine roller could lead a convoy of autonomous vehicles through hostile territory making the route safe for warfighters—while putting a minimum number of troops at risk doing so.

Oshkosh's TerraMax has participated in a bunch of U.S. government initiatives. More than a decade ago, the smart trucks were nurtured by DARPA and since then they've worked with Army, Navy and Marine Corps programs. Oshkosh Defense is pushing forward with its TerraMax unmanned ground vehicle (UGV) technology as the U.S. military eyes potential applications for such systems.

Militaries around the world continue to be interested in leader/follower smart vehicles. The U.S. Army, for example, may fund the Automated Convoy Operations program and TerraMax could win an opportunity to participate.

Technology like TerraMax could play a vital role in reducing the IED risk for U.S. warfighters in the future.

ARES – Transformer Flying Jeeps

Flying jeeps that combine 4x4 drive with a helicopter's ability to vertically take off, land and fly? We are only a few years away from tactical vehicles that both drive, and transform into something that flies, for the U.S. military.

These real life Transformers are genuinely underway and advances continue to be made at a rapid pace.

DARPA's program takes the meaning of "off-road" to entirely another level. Two of the world's top defense innovators, DARPA and Lockheed Martin's Skunk Works, are determined to deliver this capability soon.

Once upon a time this program was known as Transformer Tx, but it now goes by ARES. ARES stands for Aerial Reconfigurable Embedded System. ARES drives like a military ground vehicle and quickly transforms to fly like a helicopter—and then seamlessly can transform back again to drive tough terrain at extreme speeds.

And like Transformers, these vehicles can be operated by humans or can even fly, or drive, themselves.

Warfighters could fly or drive it into a war zone and then it could fly or drive itself back to base on autopilot....or to rendez-vous with the team somewhere else.

A hybrid helicopter and tactical ground vehicle combined into one is awesome. Who wouldn't want to drive and fly it? But it could also provide real advantages for the U.S. military.

What will a real Transformer look like?

DARPA has thrown down the gauntlet with some wow factor requirements. Here are a few of the initial challenges.

Like Transformers, this vehicle will be able to transform quickly by itself, fly by itself as well as land and take off by itself. It would even be smart enough to avoid obstacles en route and in the landing zone.

Whether flying, driving or both, ARES would have a combat range of 250 nautical miles on one tank of fuel.

To fly, ARES would transform into a Vertical Takeoff and Landing (VTOL) so that means it could lift off and land vertically—eliminating forward motion and the space that approach requires. In flight mode, it would be able to carry approximately 1,000 pounds. The cruise speed would be comparable to a light single-engine aircraft. The combat range would be similar to current helicopters.

Rather than require a certified pilot to operate the four-person vehicle, thanks in part to its automated takeoff and landing, ARES could be flown by a typical warfighter. Avoiding detection can be important in war, so ARES's takeoff, landing, and cruise would by design be quiet. DARPA challenged the team to make the new cutting-edge vehicle at least as quiet as the average car on the road. When flying, it should be at least as quiet as a single engine helicopter in the air.

On the road, the Transformer would have four-wheel drive with road performance similar to an SUV on a variety of surfaces.

And so what will it look like inside?

DARPA hopes it will have some passenger comfort while still withstanding small arms fire. Inside ARES, the design would include forward and side visibility. Each warfighter would be able to get in and out quickly under combat conditions.

Why are they important?

The U.S. increasingly relies on small combat units with transport requirements over great distances and often over rugged terrain. And ground based transportation can be dangerous.

Currently, forces generally only have two options to move around the battlespace—vehicles and helicopters. But vehicles, even heavily armored vehicles, are at risk for improvised explosive devices, ambushes and obstructions on the route. Tough terrain and roadways can not only limit movement, but can also make movements easy to track and predict by adversaries. Helicopters are another alternative, but they are in high demand with limited availability. And this option can subject air crews to another layer of threats.

Versatile, transforming vehicles could be a fantastic solution. Utilizing flight, ARES can avoid threats like ambushes and IEDs, while also allowing teams to approach targets from all sorts of directions that could give them an advantage in ground operations.

With ARES in flight mode, small units could move in and out of forward operating bases, resupply and evacuate wounded warfighters—all without having to compete with the high demand for helicopters. The team would simply utilize their own ARES vehicles.

ARES unique design could adapt to multiple missions like rapid strikes, raids and reconnaissance. It could free up limited assets, and reduce risk to personnel, by handling cargo resupply. For CASEVAC or casualty evacuation, the interior would be adaptable for one stretcher and one passenger.

The tilting ducted fans will give units the advantage of landing in far smaller landing zones—but also the opportunity to arrive and depart at faster speeds that today's helos. It is hoped ARES will give warfighters 200 knots in speed.

Even though it has all these abilities, ARES is not a behemoth. DARPA asked for ARES to be a vehicle that could readily drive down your average one-lane road and that means it needs to be about 8.5 feet wide and 30 feet long. At this size, it could be transported to war zones in C-130s and might even be stowable on small ships.

Skunk Works, one of the world's most premier and secretive defense shops, has been working with Piasecki Aircraft Corporation and AAI Corporation to achieve this feat. DARPA chose Pratt & Whitney Rocketdyne to design an engine for ARES, using their durable, lightweight, quiet EnduroCORE engine tech.

The aim is to test fly, and to test drive, the first ARES prototype in the summer of 2016. If the concept is proven, then it could become fully funded, enter production and deploy in future combat. Reportedly, the U.S. Marine Corps has taken the lead on requirements planning.

If things work out, then in the near term U.S. forces could get behind the wheel of the ultimate 4x4s that fly.

JLTV

Move over Humvee, there's a new vehicle in town that aims to combine light tank ballistic protection with Baja racer-level agility and off-road mobility in future combat.

Oshkosh Defense's JLTV will be joining the U.S. Army and Marine Corps in the battlespace. The U.S. military will have the advantage of a very capable, next-generation light vehicle that is designed to protect American troops against the threats, like IEDS, that have proliferated in today's war zones.

Next level

This new massively capable combat vehicle will be replacing the U.S. military's iconic Humvees (HMMWVS) to provide troops with even more advanced protection and off-road mobility.

With the escalation in roadside bombs and mines throughout Iraq and Afghanistan, the military sought better protection in ways like ramping up Humvees with more armor and introducing Oshkosh heavy armor MRAPS (Mine-Resistant Ambush Protected).

Troops must regularly contend with IEDs downrange and this threat will continue to be a problem. The solution? The JTLV — it has as much armor as a light tank, but still gives troops speed and agility. It will provide warfighters with better protection against this threat with improved payload and performance, and without the size of the MRAP.

Its enhanced speed means troops could travel more than 70 percent faster over rugged terrain than other standard vehicles like the M-ATV.

With its MRAP level underbody bomb protection, this new vehicle has been described as the ideal combination robust protection and off-road racing flexibility.

Features

In terms of enhanced mobility off-road, it has an adaptable suspension that can be raised and lowered with 20 inches of wheel travel. The company's TAK-4i independent suspension system is also used to provide next-generation performance.

The JLTV features shot detection, long-range surveillance, silent watch power systems as well as both visible light and IR cameras. Equipped with state-of-the-art tech, it also provides warfighters with electronic warfare devices and on-the-move battlefield situational awareness tech.

So what about the firepower? It has tube-launched missiles, remote weapons systems, as well as hands-on turret operated ones. Troop protection is paramount and the JLTV leverages the company's advances in crew protection called Oshkosh CORE1080.

There are two variants: a two-seater and a four-seater variant plus a companion trailer. The two-seat variant has one utility base vehicle platform. There are two options in the 4-seater: the General Purpose (JLTV-GP) and the Close Combat Weapons Carrier (JLTV-CCWC).

The U.S. Army Tank-automotive and Armaments Command chose Oshkosh for an approximately $6.7 billion contract to build the new Joint Light Tactical Vehicle. The competition to develop the JLTV for the military was very intense with Lockheed Martin, AM General, and Oshkosh—all with outstanding designs—as the final three.

JLTV production is already underway with the first deliveries expected for the second half of 2016.

HELLHOUND

How about a vehicle...with a laser weapon?

While civilian vehicles come with options like a custom paint job or special upholstery, Hellhound has been designed as laser-optional. Military users can opt for an integrated 10-kilowatt solid-state fiber laser.

If an ATV and an armored fighting vehicle had a baby, it may very well look, and drive, like the Hellhound. This new, sleek, black vehicle can drive fast and furious into enemy battlespace on missions, all while protected with smart armor— and equipped with a laser.

Hellhound aims to bring laser weapons—once the stuff of science fiction—directly into future battlefields and put that power directly into the hands of warfighters. Made by Northrop Grumman, the six-and-a-half ton Hellhound can carry a driver, five passengers— and the aforementioned laser weapon.

Laser weapons

To fire that laser, it needs a lot of power. Hellhound packs an immense amount of power into a compact size.

A 10 kW laser weapons could theoretically defeat enemy UAVs, vehicles, aircraft, rockets, artillery, mortars, and more. Unlike traditional vehicle weapons systems, a team in the laser-equipped Hellhound would never run out of "ammo," as long as there is power that magazine stays deep.

This next-gen vehicle generates so much power that when it is applied for humanitarian purposes in a war zone...Hellhound can make a significant difference. One practical example in a humanitarian disaster scenario would be a blackout. If there is a power blackout, the Hellhound can singlehandedly power an entire field hospital so that it can keep on running. Or in support of military operations...if an enemy attacks the power supply to a command center, the Hellhound could provide the power to keep it going.

In addition to the laser, the vehicle can also be ramped up with an EOS Technologies R-400 Remote Weapon Station, an ATK M230LF 30mm cannon, and a swing-arm weapon mount.

So how's the ride?

The Hellhound is transportable in the Boeing CH-47 Chinook helicopter and could unload and drive straight into the war zone. It is designed to perform in the most rugged of conditions consistent with what U.S. military reconnaissance missions may face.

With 4-wheel drive, Hellhound harnesses the 250HP Cummins engine and leverages the six speed Allison transmission. To make that ultra rough terrain seem as easy as a well-paved city street, the vehicle utilizes Fox Defense advanced shock absorbers.

Often reconnaissance work can involve rugged terrain and a brush with enemy bullets—both of which can be tough on tires. But Hellhound includes a number of smart ways to tackle threats to tires. Tech like the Meritor Central Tire Inflation System keeps tires at the right pressure and reduces wear and tear. Correct pressure can translate into better fuel economy, and longer mission endurance, without refueling.

Punctured tires? Not a problem. Hellhound will keep on going. Flat wheel tech allows the vehicle to drive out of harm's way in spite of a flat.

The laser race

As discussed in the *Weapons* section of this book, the race to field laser weapons continues to intensify with the U.S. military and many top companies advancing, and competing, in this space. Making lasers actually work on vehicles like this represents a crucial step in taking laser weapons from science fiction to a reality on the battlefield.

Ultimately, lasers could become an optional upgrade for not just military vehicles, but aircraft and ships as well.

TERRIER – Swiss Army Knife of Combat Tractors

Tractors aren't just handy at home. They're also in demand for war and the tractors of future combat are hardcore multi-taskers.

BAE Systems' Terrier is affectionately known as the Swiss Army Knife of combat vehicles because there isn't anything it can't tackle. A multi-tool on a giant scale, the Terrier is a number of critical vehicles all in one. It can quickly adapt to tackle a range of important tasks. It even has a 26-foot arm.

So what can this battle tractor do? The 32-ton armored combat vehicle is an ultimate tractor— one that can punch holes through concrete, fire rockets, and carve safe passage through minefields for warfighters.

Terrier can destroy enemy runways, rip holes in concrete compounds where terrorists hide, and dismantle bridges.

This mammoth machine beast can even unleash PYTHON rocket-propelled explosives to destroy concealed IEDS, protecting dismounted troops.

What else can it do?

Like tractors found all throughout the United States, Terrier can lift, grab and move things. But the Terrier is next level: its front loader system can lift five tons.

It can move a staggering 300 tons of earth per hour— that's about the weight of 120 5,000-pound SUVs.

Terrier can deploy its excavator arm and bucket to destroy bridges, obstacles, and more. In both day and night conditions, the vehicle's cameras provide 360-degree vision.

In spite of weighing a mammoth 32 tons, Terrier can reach speeds of more than 45 miles per hour. Off-roading is no problem for Terrier, and it can even execute missions that require travelling through water and braving six-foot waves.

This cutting-edge tractor can be run by remote control from about 3300 feet away.

Defeating bombs

So it can shift an enormous amount of weight— but that's just the beginning of its talents in war zones.

In the battlespace, IEDs remains a serious, ongoing threat. Terrier can help defeat this threat and play a key role in keeping military, aid personnel, and civilians safe.

Terrier's telescopic investigation arm extends over more than 26 feet from the vehicle. This long arm allows warfighters to probe and unearth buried, dangerous devices from a safe distance.

A special IED-focused plow—like a massive cattle guard— can also be quickly attached to Terrier to defeat this threat.

Hammer, ripper and auger

The highly adaptive Terrier is packed with features. Terriers can now also come equipped with a rock hammer, ripper and earth auger.

The hammer can split rocks and even penetrate concrete. Its ripper can tear up roads or runways. How is that useful downrange? One example would be preventing enemy use of transportation routes.

And for combat engineering tasks, the Terrier's earth auger can drill holes.

Wet work

BAE System's new advancements mean the Terrier will also be able to wade through much deeper waters. It will even be able to withstand wave surges that are even bigger than six feet.

For combat, the surge protection and the deeper wading mean the Terrier can be even more useful in coastal and other low-lying areas. Beyond combat, the enhanced wading will mean better support in humanitarian aid and disaster response like hurricane, flooding and tsunami devastated regions.

BAE Systems designed the Terrier to provide the British Army with maximum flexibility from a single vehicle. Terrier's all in one, streamlined approach means the military can reduce the massive equipment they need downrange and just bring one vehicle to do the jobs of several.

FAST AND LIGHT

SILENT HAWK AND THE NIGHTMARE

Ultra stealth, futuristic motorcycles are underway to let forces travel silent and fast. Two new hybrid motorcycles, Silent Hawk and the NightMare, are excellent for special operations work.

While many love the sound of a roaring chopper...when working downrange it can be less than ideal. A cutting-edge motorcycle that is fast, rugged, stealthy and silent could be a great advantage for missions—particularly for SOF work.

Hybrids could also bring to the fight an amazing ability to harvest all sorts of things downrange and use it as fuel. On a mission, fuel might not be readily available and this provides a fantastic opportunity to make use of whatever might be around.

A field expedient, silent, fast motorcycle—how can you not love that?

Coming soon

And American warfighters could very soon field a two-wheel-drive hybrid with these talents. Within a mere two years, the concept has gone from idea to prototype.

In 2014, DARPA launched a program to develop a military-use, hybrid motorcycle that will operate nearly silently in electric mode. DARPA funded two teams for phase two development under a small business innovative research award: The Silent Hawk by Alta Motors with Logos and the Nightmare from LSA Autonomy.

Both bikes can each run for at least 120 miles on combined electric and heavy fuel sources and reach top speeds of about 80 miles per hour. Instead of conventional rear-wheel drive only, both bikes feature a front-wheel motor and rear motors. This is a great design choice for extreme off-road.

Silent Hawk and NightMare leverage futuristic, hybrid multi-fuel engines that can run on a surprising range of all sorts of combustibles. It is expected that it could be anything from bog standard gasoline and BBQ propane through to jet fuel and stuff on your kitchen shelf. In conversations with operators, they've hinted the tech is so advanced that they could run the bike on things sourced by rummaging around their kitchens...I haven't personally tried fueling one up with olive oil to confirm that—yet. Stay tuned on that front.

How quiet is quiet?

Speed and stealth are crucial when approaching the enemy, and current motorcycles are less than ideal because of the noise they generate. Raids, for example, can require infiltration into an area. If this can be done more quietly, then it can be a benefit to the operation.

Ideally, the hybrid will be silent in electric mode and very quiet when operating on fuel.

When the bikes are running in quiet mode they use battery systems. In this quiet mode, the noise is kept down remarkably to about 55 decibels. That is not quiet like quiet in a very quiet library—but it is as quiet as indoor conversation in a quiet suburb which is about 55 decibels. That degree of quiet is ace for travelling fast in a stealthy and undetected way.

When running on regular fuel, the bikes are about 80 decibels. That's about as loud as your typical dishwasher.

While down in Tampa for meetings at SOCOM this year, I had a chance to get personal with both prototypes since they'd been brought down for SOF folks to see. Operators would get a whole lot of use—and a whole lot of fun—out of the rugged, lightweight, two-wheel-drive off-road motorcycles DARPA has challenged the two companies to create. They readily won my vote as truly bad ass.

SILENT HAWK

To create the Silent Hawk, two small innovative American companies Logos Technologies and Alta Motors, teamed together to leverage the former's expertise in hybrid power projects and the latter's in creating state-of-the-art electric motorcycles.

The Silent Hawk bike uses a drone propulsion system in hybrid mode. Logos first designed the hybrid-electric propulsion system for unmanned aircraft. Now it is being leveraged on the ground.

This hybrid system has been integrated into the Alta Motors' off-road dirt electric RedShift MX. Enthusiasts rave about Alta Motor's Redshift. It features 40 horse-power and weighs about 250 pounds. It is one of the fastest, publicly available electric dual-sport bikes currently available.

The electric system for Silent Hawk has been created by Alta Motors. The ultra high intensity battery pack even has a cooling system that utilizes a multicell approach—kind of like Teslas.

DARPA set a tough challenge. Developing an engine that is powerful, small enough to fit on a bike with a rugged battery is not easy. The Alta Motors solution is a compact-battery pack with 180 watt-hours per kilogram, similar to a laptop battery, but tough enough to withstand off-road missions.

In quiet mode, the SilentHawk can run for up to two hours on a single charge. The multi-fuel generator can be turned on and that extends the range to a combined distance of 170 miles. When the generator is on, Silent Hawk is not as quiet as silent mode—but it is still quieter than the average motorcycle, which is about 80 to 100 decibels. With the generator on, it is approximately 75 decibels and that's about as loud as vacuum cleaner.

If only the silent mode is required for an urgent mission, then operators can easily detach the hybrid version and swap in the electric-only approach. The bike's hybrid-electric unit fits under the seat and can be rapidly attached, or detached, from the bike.

What does hybrid mean on a practical level? Longer range on missions, for sure. As long as the operator can scrounge something with some smart field expediency, then this futuristic hybrid engine will keep the bike running as long as an operator needs it to. Whether it is conventional fuel, diesel, jet, propane or even biofu-el...such a wide range is compatible so the Silent Hawk can take it and keep on going.

And get this, the Silent Hawk is so advanced it can figure out what you've fueled it up with and automatically adjust to harness that specific fuel.

Off-road

Alta Motors' bikes are very robust. Operators who have used them have described them to me as truly being tough enough to take being dumped, dropped, slid, tipped, and just plain crashed. Admittedly, I may have done my utmost to smash one up to no avail. There's no question they are very robust machines.

Soft soil and narrow, steep trails found in war zones can be difficult to quickly tackle, and that's one of the reasons DARPA is developing two-wheel-drive vehicles that will be able to travel substantial distances, on extremely challenging terrain, more easily.

The all terrain versatility would also come in handy for staying off the roads and routes that are 4-wheel vehicle accessible and therefore may be anticipated. With Silent Hawk, operators could take unpredictable off-road routes through wooded, or other tough terrain, giving them a number of tactical advantages.

Silence and easy transportability are two other key advantages important to stress. Take a scenario where a SOF team is inserted by a helicopter, then needs to rapidly and stealthily close in on a target—the bike's silent mode and speed could be very convenient to avoid detection and ensure surprise. Silent Hawk could also prove useful in reaching a second landing zone for an easy extraction with the nimble, small, light weight bikes easily boarding some helicopters.

As warfare continues to require the deployment of small units to remote and extreme terrains, technology like the Silent Hawk allow U.S. forces to do more with less.

And it will provide more than a way to travel; the bike would be a portable electric power source, thus reducing the need to lug heavy batteries into the field. The Silent Hawk could provide 7.5 kilowatts for running external devices.

THE NIGHTMARE

The NightMare is larger than the Silent Hawk and weighs approximately 400 pounds. Made by LSA Autonomy, it has more horsepower with 17 in front and 135 in back. It averages around 13 kilowatts in generated power.

To make that level of power work and fit on a small, lightweight rugged frame, LSA Autonomy took the approach of building a motorcycle chassis from scratch around its hybrid engine. As part of their design, they've used a belt instead of a chain to further reduce engine noise.

In addition to special operations work, hybrid bikes could be useful for a range of other purposes, including scouting, convoy control and military policing.

While the silent mode of both bikes is only near truly silent so far...DARPA has helped hybrid electric bikes advance remarkably quickly in two short years.

PEGASUS – the Flying Dune Buggy

Does a flying dune buggy sound like fun? For France's Special Operations Forces, it's a new way to get to work.

Pegasus, Vaylon's flying dune buggy, combines all-terrain buggy and what's described as a "micro-light" aircraft. It is designed to take off and fly in powered flight or paraglide. In French, it is called Pegase. And in either language, it is named after the flying horse of Greek mythology.

The flying dune buggy was created as a solution to undetected approach. When special operations forces approach by helicopter, the helo generates noise and this can give advance warning to enemy forces. The flying buggy, however, can take off under powered flight, fly 3,000 meters or more, and then silently glide to a target as opposed to the noisy helo approach.

Pegasus is intended to deploy on a range of missions from hostage rescue and recon through to equipment transport and air drop required for difficult to reach targets. When the Pegasus project was announced, I was in Paris and the French military shared a video of some of the special operations teams flying the combination hang glider-dune buggy. Suffice it to say, it looked like a whole lot of fun. The prototype was unveiled at the biennial Eurosatory, one of the largest weapons and land warfare showcases in the world. In the Direction Générale de l'Armement (DGA) VIP area where it was cosseted, I had a chance to get a close look at it. It's not everyday you get to sit in a flying a dune buggy (sadly stationary) with a seemingly endless supply of excellent champagne filling one's glass. Since I wasn't going to fly it that trip, I wanted to hear the French SOF opinion of its performance and how it would be further modified to enhance military use. The short answer is: it works. And yes, it is a blast.

So what can it do?

Pegasus, a hybrid combining a dune buggy with and an ultra light aircraft, can fly to more than 10,000 feet. In the air, it can travel at speeds between 35 to 50 miles per hour.

It has STOL (Short Take Off and Landing)—meaning it requires less than 330 feet to take off and it can land in under 330 feet too—even on poorly prepared fields. It's designed to provide access to tough spots—overcoming rivers, dunes, cliffs, damaged roads and more to give operators quick and silent access.

Two people can travel in the vehicle and can stay aloft in the air up to three hours. The vehicle's silent propellers ensure a stealthy approach. It can carry up to approximately 550 pounds.

On the road it can reach up to about 65 mph and can manage both dry and wet surfaces.

Pegasus may ultimately also be armed with weapons, ranging from machine guns to light multi-role missiles. The passenger seat would be removable to provide space for combat kit like weapons and equipment for a mission. The company plans on letting French Special Operations Forces direct them in what would best meet their requirements.

The prototype uses petrol for fuel, but later evolutions will most likely use diesel fuel since it can be easier for the military.

How would it be used?

Compact and light, Pegasus would be air-transportable and droppable. This is a key advantage because it can make rapid access to hard-to-reach places easier. In addition to rapid deployment, it has also been designed to provide a speedy - yet quiet - approach to support fast intervention on the ground.

Beyond combat applications, the vehicle could also be used to reach hard to reach civilians in the aftermath of natural disasters. It could even be used for tourism.

In 2012, the French Direction Générale de l'Armement funded the Pegasus prototype's development to the tune of more than $80,000 for the French Special Operations Forces. Like all SOF, France's forces have a requirement for all-terrain vehicles and for creative ways to approach undetected. The vehicle underwent extensive trials with the country's military over the past few years.

What's next?

A new, lighter Mk2 version is under development. Rather than carrying the crew side-by-side, it carries them in tandem with the intention of lowering the vehicle's profile. It also has two engines: one is for flying and the other is for driving on the road.

While Vaylon, aims to make Pegasus widely available to commercial users too, interested civilians may be looking at a possible price tag of more than $100,00 for a single Pegasus.

MRZRS

Who doesn't love an all-terrain vehicle? U.S. Special Operations Command (SOCOM) is no exception. The latest and greatest in pimped-out ATVs designed for Special Operations just got even better.

Polaris is well known for their excellent ATVs and their popular models can be found all over America. But what may be less well known is that the company also has a team that focuses on creating top notch ATVs for military purposes too. In 2016, Polaris Defense revealed a new high-performance MRZR turbo diesel (MRZR-D) that will be joining its stable of state-of-the art off-road vehicles.

The ultra-light MRZRs have long been a military favorite for their excellent off-road mobility. They are easily configurable and allow operators to quickly prepare for missions and then tackle the most extreme terrain with maximum flexibility. In addition to the U.S., more than 20 allied countries rely on MRZRs to meet mission demands..

On certain missions and areas of operation, diesel may be more readily available, so this change will provide more flexibility. MRZRs are also easily transportable via tactical aircraft to wherever in the world they are needed— another key feature that makes them very fit for the purpose of SOF work.

What's new?

For years, I've seen firsthand that Polaris Defense actively gathers and listens to feedback from operators and incorporates it into development. During the past three years, SOCOM provided lots of feedback on how they were using MRZRs and what enhancements could help them complete their missions more effectively. Polaris Defense again listened closely and then made those advances happen in the new vehicle.

The enhancements include refinements such as better sightlines, occupant seating space and ergonomics. The MRZR-D also has even better range and more auxiliary power. Features such as handling, dimensions, payload and ground clearance have remained the same.

Have Aircraft will Travel

Like the MRZRs, the MRZR-D vehicles can be transported downrange with V-22 helicopters. They can be configured a range of ways—including for two-, four- and six-person teams.

Once on land, off-road capability can be essential for U.S. Special Operations folks to execute many types of missions so the MRZRs can provide lots of advantages. One advantage is that the vehicle's ruggedness broadens access to remote locations. MRZRs allow teams to move faster and lighter with more gear. By reducing the weight they need to carry and shifting the work to the MRZR-D, warfighter combat fatigue can also be reduced and performance optimized.

These Special Operations-optimized ATVs feature on-demand advanced all-wheel drive. When more traction is needed, the vehicle automatically engages all four wheels and can automatically revert back to two-wheel. This advanced technology translates into more power when an operator needs it on a mission and also less general wear and tear on the vehicle.

The MRZR-D 2 can carry 1,000 pounds while the MRZR-D 4 can carry 1,500. Both variants also reach about 60 mph maximum speed with 88 HP engines that have been designed for extreme performance in the toughest terrain. The vehicles have fantastic throttle response and acceleration. In addition, they have standard features like a winch, aircraft tie-downs, large cargo boxes and fold-down rollover structures for operator protection.

To ensure maximum agility, the ATVs are built with a low center of gravity. In part, this is achieved by cunning placement of key components like the engine. The vehicles also have keyless ignition, which makes it easy to jump in and go when every second counts.

The smooth, highly responsive electronic power steering can help reduce fatigue for operators that have to drive for very long periods. The roll cage has a smart design that provides protection, but can be quickly and easily removed without tools.

From your backyard to downrange

In 2015, the U.S. military decided to buy more of the very popular Polaris Defense all-terrain vehicles that are very similar to the ATVs that you and your friends might drive—just amped up for military purposes as we looked at above.

USSOCOM awarded Polaris Defense an $83 million, five-year deal for more MRZR 2s and MRZR 4s.

Polaris Defense had been supplying its MRZR ATVs to SOCOM for a while—and now U.S. Special Operations will be getting their hands on even more. Ultra-light vehicle mobility will continue to be a key capability for U.S. Special Operations missions. And the Polaris ATVs are outstanding—best in class for sure. Every time I get to drive or ride, I can't help but be impressed with the MRZRs. Words don't do them justice, they need to be experienced to fully appreciate what they bring to the fight. I'm besotted with them. If you love your Polaris ATV at home, then you'd have a blast with the military versions.

Production of the vehicles will continue for USSOCOM and other international contracts.

ROBOTS

ROBOT OPPOSING FORCES

Millions of rounds can be fired at a new breed of robot and they'll keep on going. These robots can survive in part because they have state of the art armor, but also because they can think and behave like special operations teams—and avoid getting shot. These robots can even learn to behave like human enemy forces.

Robots that think, communicate with each other and fight as a team will play a role in future land combat. Militaries around the world, including the United States, continue to advance robotics for warfare.

Robotic Opposing Force (ROPFOR), comprised of Marathon Target-made robots, can replicate the tactical maneuvers of any human enemy force on the battlefield.

They may not look humanoid, but they possess AI — that's Artificial Intelligence — so just like human military teams they can think, act, react, work together, evolve and communicate in response to their environment and human military teams.

While it may sound like the stuff of *Rise of the Machines*, these robots are currently used for advanced training — not for deployment to battlefields. The technology is not there yet for humanoid combat machines like the Terminators. But the AI on these robots could play a role in paving the way in the evolution of Terminator-style tech.

Special Operations Forces around the world have been leveraging the human-like abilities of the cutting-edge Marathon Target robots to enhance their skills. They are used to challenge—and sharpen—a warfighter's response to dynamic and evolving tactical situations.

By going up against these robot teams, small units have the chance to work against thinking targets that will act unexpectedly and unpredictably like human threats.

This is a modern way to train, but also a great way to rehearse missions—whether it is a hostage rescue or the capture of a terrorist.

How does it work?

In urban operations training, the robots play the role of the enemy — an enemy that can think and work as a team to challenge the latest human assault team tactics and techniques.

For assault forces approaching an urban target, the robots' AI helps simulate a realistic and tough enemy. As just one example for snipers, the robots can be used for them to challenge themselves when working from urban hides. Or to challenge snipers working from helicopters to practice aerial target engagement with thinking, adapting and reacting behavior that replicate real bad guy responses.

The robots may not have legs, but they very effectively simulate how humans move during close-quarter battle. A robot can alternate speeds—one minute traveling at a sprint, then standing still, and breaking back into a run. Like humans in combat, they will also move in unpredictable directions.

For combat scenarios with a mix of civilians, friendly forces and enemy forces, the robots can be dressed accordingly. In these situations, the robots will also react like civilians. If you take a hostage mission, for example, the 'hostage' robot could react to a rescue in any number of real ways whether sinking to the ground crying or bolting off in an inconvenient direction.

In every scenario, terrorists are not going to conveniently behave like the widely used stationary paper or predictable track targets. The robots can play a vital role in sharpening warfighters' threat discrimination and rules of engagement.

Why aren't they humanoid?

The technology is not there yet. And for training purposes, it doesn't need to be.

In addition to marksmanship training, the robots are excellent for mission practice in urban settings and are frequently used to practice room clearing. However, there are limitations—they can't climb stairs yet, so robots have to be placed in advance on other floors and are limited to movement on those floors.

Nonetheless, the robots can manage uneven, wooded terrain and that's handy for snipers training on those scenarios. The robots look like human shaped targets when observed at range.

Taking convoy protection as one skill set example to sharpen, the robots can also be taught how the enemy behaves... so the robots will replicate how the enemy conducts movements, formations and rendezvous. This way, snipers can refine their target acquisition skills in advance.

When I was down at Fort Bragg for the USASOC International Sniper Competition this year, I watched top SOF sniper teams from around the United States, and the world, go up against the robots. There is no question the robots presented a unique, unexpected, interesting challenge for the top notch talent. I also shot against them at Fort Bragg with some of the SF operators and we were all impressed. In fact one of the most skilled, agile and fit operators I've ever come across, pulled a muscle trying to keep up with them. We all found this extremely hilarious, but it proves the point that the robots can help get you out of routines and habits while keeping operators truly challenged and engaged.

It is a whole lot more challenging than a paper target.

DECEPTION-BOTS

Future robots could deceive not just other robots, but human adversaries—and this could be thanks to devious behavior common in nature. Using deceptive behavioral patterns of squirrels and birds, researchers at the Georgia Institute of Technology have successfully developed robots that are able to deceive each other.

Squirrels are nefarious tricksters. They gather acorns, store them in specific location and then routinely return to patrol the hidden caches. If a hungry squirrel sidles up for a raid on the caches, the nut owner will visit empty acorn sites to deceive the would-be squirrel acorn-nicker.

Could robots be just as clever?

The Georgia Tech School of Interactive Computing professor took this crafty squirrel strategy and applied it to robots. Ronald Arkin's detailed research, funded by the

Office of Naval Research, was published IEEE Intelligent Systems in 2012.

The robot succeeded in luring a "predator" robot to a fake location, delaying the exposure and seizure of the resources it was tasked to protect.

Applied to the battlespace, robots could practice the military art of deception by reacting to scenarios in the moment—rather than a human directing them in what to do and how to respond. Take a scenario where a robot was assigned to guard an ammunition cache on the battlefield. When the robot became aware an enemy was nearby, the robot could change its patrolling strategies to deceive another intelligent robot hunting for it. Or it could even deceive human recon teams. It could decide that it must adapt and deceive in order to gain time for human reinforcements.

Bluffing like a bird

Arkin and student Justin Davis also created a simulation and demo based on birds that might bluff their way to safety.

When there is a threat of an attack, Arabian babbler birds will sometimes opt to launch a mob counterattack. The Arabian babbler will band up with other birds to harass the predator until it finally surrenders and departs.

The team researched whether a robot equipped with the babbling bird bluff would be more likely to survive. Their research showed this deception technique was the best approach — provided there were enough robots to create a group large enough to harass a predator into departing.

In the event this minimum threshold could be reached, the gain outweighed the risk of the robot deception being exposed.

How does this translate to military applications? If a robot is under threat, then it could bluff and feign it is fierce enough to defeat an adversary—even though the robot might not be able to protect itself at all. When confronted with the threat, the robot would understand that if the robot is forthcoming about its lack of any lethal capabilities or authorized use of force, then it could lead to capture or destruction. It would intuitively understand that its best chance of survival and mission completion would be to bluff.

Also funded by the Office of Naval Research, Georgia Tech researchers made another key breakthrough in robot deception. This project laid the groundwork for robots independently deciding whether to deceive another intelligent machine or human. Essentially, this earlier work helped to pave the way for robots to independently decide to evade and hide from the enemy and independently engage in activities like creating a false trail to prevent capture by an enemy combatant, whether another robot or human.

Deception in war

If military robots were to employ deception, it would hardly be the first subterfuge in warfare. One readily familiar deception technique is concealment. Camouflage material is a form of concealment, designed to mislead an adversary by making a warfighter, or vehicle, more difficult to identify.

Like AI, equipping robots with the ability to deceive each other — not to mention humans — is a charged ethical issue that could expect some heated debate in future combat planning.

SELF-ASSEMBLING ROBOTS – M-Blocks

Is an army of *Terminator II* style shape-shifting androids — ones that can self-assemble, self-repair and transform — finally possible?

An American team proved that they have laid the foundation for self-assembling robot swarms that can self-configure for a mission. It is truly astonishing stuff.

Announced in 2013, the small cubes called M-Blocks were created by an MIT team led by Computer Science and Artificial Intelligence Laboratory research scientist John Romanishin. M-Blocks look like cubes slightly bigger than those that make up a Rubik's Cube. They have no visible parts — yet they still manage to launch themselves forward.

They can leap into the air, roll, and even climb over and around one another. Suspended upside-down from metallic surfaces, they can still move. Ultimately, M-blocks can use these maneuvers to jump onto each other to build a required shape—sort of like a robotic real-life Tetris.

Modular robot systems like the M-block could lead to microbot swarms that can self-assemble, like the shapeshifting T-1000 in *Terminator II*. But beyond becoming robots for war, this sort of technology also has wide potential beyond defense.

In the event of a biological or chemical attack, the robot swarms could enter and investigate dangerous environments reducing risk to human life. They could then transform themselves into tech solutions for the crisis. And that is just one example of many.

How it works

If M-Blocks don't have any external mechanisms, how do they move and assemble?

Inside each M-Block is a flywheel that can achieve speeds of 20,000 revolutions per minute. When this flywheel brakes, it provides the momentum to move. Each face and edge of an M-Block has magnets that attach one cube to another. On each edge there are two cylindrical magnets and on each cube face are four magnet pairs. When a moving cube lands on another, these help it snap into place.

These cubes can literally fly through the air from any direction and the magnets then align when they land. The cubes' edges are also beveled, so if a cube begins to flip on top of another, the bevels and magnets touch. As cubes approach each other, their magnets rotate aligning opposite poles, north with south, creating a strong connection and anchoring the pivot.

This is certainly not the only project working on paving the way towards Terminator T-1000s, but other complicated, high-tech solutions have failed in their pursuit of self-assembling robots. This team's success is in part due to their deploy a low-tech solution.

Often in these self-assembling robot projects, an individual piece can't move by itself like an M-Block. And on a practical level, if a block got separated from its team then it couldn't rejoin them. Not so with the M-blocks. These little guys can make their way back to their team by themselves and rejoin.

Amazingly, these cubes can operate as a team in what is called "cooperative group behavior."

In practice, this means that multiple cubes can work together to move other cubes and even drag assembled cube structures.

Further down the development road, cubes could be equipped to provide special tools ranging from lights and cameras through to battery packs. The MIT researchers are working on building an army of cubes, each able to move in any direction and leverage new algorithms to guide them.

Ultimately, thousands of cubes could be scattered about and yet still be able to identify each other, coalesce, and configure into a required shape entirely by themselves.

SELF-DESTRUCTING ELECTRONICS (VAPR)

After a mission is completed, it can be very difficult to track and recover every electronic device that was used. There is always a risk that gadgets left on the battlefield could be captured by an enemy or found by a local and sold to an adversary. Once in unfriendly hands, the advanced technology could compromise the U.S. military's strategic technological advantage.

What if electronics simply vanished when they were no longer needed? Radios, sensors and other electronic devices that self-destruct and vanish on command may soon be in the hands of American forces.

DARPA's Vanishing Programmable Resources (VAPR) program intends to develop "transient electronics": Gear just as robust and functional as current electronics that can dissolve and disappear into the environment when triggered—think next gen self-destruct.

Even if left on the battlefield, VAPR electronics would be useless if they ended up in enemy hands. It would also prevent enemies, or clients of enemies, from copying the innovation and then using it against U.S. forces.

The Agency reached out to companies to help the military devise solutions. They're looking for solutions to break down the electronics — beyond simply dunking the electronics in water. As well as solutions to other key components like how to trigger the novel method of break down. Break down could be triggered in a range of ways from a signal or the application of heat through to lots of options not suitable for public disclosure.

Current degradable electronics methods tend to use polymers and biologically-derived materials. However, both produce limited results due to their poor electronic and sometimes weak mechanical properties. An ideal solution to "transient" electronics would add this new breakdown and vanish ability—but while ensuring the electronics perform at a state of the art level.

If successful, in future combat there could be a revolutionary new class of electronics—ones that self-destruct without a trace.

CYBORGS

NESD

Could the U.S. deploy 'cyborg' troops? The U.S. military is working to develop a new chip technology that, when implanted, will connect human brains to computers—in a way it would make the warfighters into cyborgs.

What's a cyborg? By definition, a cyborg is a person whose physical abilities are extended beyond normal human limitations by mechanical elements built into the body.

DARPA often plays a big role in the development of technologies that civilians eventually benefit from, such as GPS or the Internet. The Agency recently revealed the new Neural Engineering System Design, or NESD, program. By investing in research, DARPA hopes to create an implantable neural interface that will connect humans directly to computers at an unprecedented level.

Should the chip succeed, it could have nearly limitless possibilities.

For the U.S. military, it could help warfighters on a number of levels, such as augmenting their senses—hearing, sight and more.

The technology has the potential to restore sight to the blind, transform prosthetics into limbs that function seamlessly like the original one. It is hoped that NESD could even possibly control disease.

NESD falls within President Obama's Brain Research through Advancing Innovative Neurotechnologies (BRAIN) initiative launched in 2013. BRAIN is intended to encourage research that will cure, or help, brain disorders and brain damage.

How does it work?

The new chip will be about the size of sugar cube or two stacked nickels– that's about one cubic centimeter.

NESD will act as a translator between the brain and digital world. The brain neurons use one language and computers another.

The chip would be implanted in the brain. Once implanted, it will act as a neural interface. Its job is to convert electrochemical signals sent by neurons in the brain. The chip will translate these brain signals into the ones and zeros that computers understand and then translate the computer messages into signals the brain understands.

Currently, human-computer interface tech connects a machine to approximately 100 to 1,000 neurons at a time.

With this revolutionary chip, the tech will connect individual neurons to the machine. And potentially it will be able to so with millions of them in the future.

Why does this matter? By leveraging individual neuron connections, the user would enjoy far better and finer control, a reduction in noise and accelerated communication between the human and the linked computer.

So how, for example, would it improve the user's vision? The computer would feed the brain additional digital visual information that augments the user's sense of sight.

For a civilian whose sight is impaired—the computer would feed the brain the additional data, helping to restore the sight so that they can "see."

For the warfighter, think feeding visual data in a higher resolution than is currently possible. Seeing much farther away with data overlays. Maybe even potentially augmenting them to "see" inside things and through things with Superman-style vision. The tech could possibly unlock other capabilities like the option to use the human eye to see through the bird's eye view of a drone "looking" at a terrorist training camp around the bend—and then the warfighter by merely thinking it, could switch back to what the naked eye sees to brief the team on what he "saw" and how it impacts planning. Back at headquarters, Commanders could theoretically "see" through the eyes of warfighter as what they see projects on a display.

Why haven't cyborgs been successful yet?

Current human neural interfaces squash massive amounts of data through about 100 channels. Each of these channels then aggregates signals from thousands of neurons. This approach means you get an outcome that is messy and noisy.

NESD aims to create a system that solves these problems. The groundbreaking tech will allow clear and individual communication with any one of the neurons—and up to an extraordinary one million neurons—in a given region of the brain at any time.

The current quality of systems that interface the human brain with a computer have been described by experts in this stuff to me like this—its been like trying to get two ultra advanced supercomputers to communicate with each other using the rudimentary modems you'd use at home. Less than ideal. So one of the goals with this project is to advance the way the brain can connect with computers so that they can talk to each other in an unrestricted way.

Next steps

DARPA hopes the chip will be part of wider series of advances. For full NESD potential to be achieved, it will require further breakthroughs. Some of the additional advances necessary would be in medical device manufacturing and packaging, synthetic biology, neuroscience, low-power electronics and photonics.

Thanks to NESD, humans could be connecting with computers in an unprecedented way in the not so distant future. Imagine a world where you think to interact with your computer and devices, rather than type or speak. A future where thought replaces keystrokes. But more importantly, NESD holds immediate promise to restore limbs to warfighters and civilians alike. In the near term, it could enable prosthetics to respond and react to thought just like natural limbs.

The NESD program is expected to start yielding results by 2020.

MARITIME

UNDERWATER

SHORTFIN BARRACUDA

Mega stealth, ultra state of the art and jam-packed with advanced next-gen tech and weaponry...this new fleet of Shortfin Barracuda Block 1A submarines will bring decisive power to any fight. A key ally to the United States, Australia, is ramping up their military might with $39 billion in futuristic submarines.

French company DCNS is developing these new, cutting-edge Shortfin Barracudas for the Royal Australian Navy. The project will be a collaboration between Australia and France—but the United States is also expected to play a vital role.

DCNS will be leveraging the state-of-the-art technology originally created for its big brother—the French Navy's Barracuda attack submarine.

The powerful French subs are aptly named after the Barracuda fish that tends to incite fear with its large size and scary predatory look. Rapid and powerful, it is a smart, formidable hunter known to deploy clever tactics like working together to drive fish into shallow water to trap them.

Naturally lean and stealthy, barracudas excel at stalking targets hidden from their sight until they strike—just like these mega stealth submarines. So why is the new sub called Shortfin Barracuda? Shortfins are native to Australia's Great Barrier Reef.

And while many details remain confidential and shrouded in secrecy, DCNS, France and Australia have revealed some key elements. Here's what we know...

Missions

Capable of conducting missions for about 80 days straight, a crew of 60—and possibly more than 20 SOF operators—will be able to fit into the approximately 320 foot long sub.

The big brother Barracuda's design has a hatch that can hold up to eight SOF Operators for insertion and extraction missions. It is likely that the Shortfin will include a similar feature.

The Shortfin can deep dive to depths of 1150 feet and when it dives, it displaces more than 4,000 tons.

Speed and Propulsion

The Shortfin Barracuda has a top speed of more than 20 knots—that's 23 miles per hour. During operations, the new sub can cover 18,000 nautical miles at 10 knots or 11.5 mph and this will be particularly useful for Australia's patrolling of vast ocean distances.

To reach these speeds and such range, the Shortfin Barracuda relies on modern propulsion. The sub's pump jet propulsion replaces the old school obsolete propeller tech found on many fleets around the world. The French version is nuclear powered, however Australia has opted for diesel-electric propulsion.

Shortfin's hydroplanes will be able to retract and this plays a role in helping to reduce both drag and noise. The quieter a sub is...the harder it is for bad guys to find it.

Stealth

One of the key features is the Shortfin Barracuda's stealth capability. Shortfin will leverage state-of-the-art tech that dramatically reduces signature.

In a rather landmark decision, France is offering Australia access to their advanced-stealth tech. This is tech that was designed for their top-tier platforms like their nuclear-powered general-purpose attack submarines and their ballistic missile submarines.

DCNS has suggested that the Shortfin Barracuda will also be equipped with the world's most powerful sonar ever produced for a conventional submarine.

Weapons

Australia's Defence Force could deploy the Shortfins as intelligence-gathering platforms, but also as a forceful deterrent that stealthily patrols vast distances armed with state of the art weapons systems.

The Shortfin weaponry could include French heavyweight DCNS's F21 torpedoes and sea mines. In terms of missiles, it could also be armed with French DCNS's Exocets (Flying Fish) to launch against ships. To defend against air threats from aircraft like helicopters and drones, it could possibly also be armed with DCNS's A3SMs.

But it is also expected that the United States will also play a role in Australia's new subs, particularly in providing weapons and integrated combat systems.

The Shortfin Barracuda will replace several Australian Navy Collins subs that will reach retirement age in about a decade. During the selection process, the Shortfin beat out Japan's Soryu-class and German firm TKMS' Type-

216. The Collins will need to stay in service for another several years until the Shortfins are ready. The Shortfins are expected to be operational in the early 2030s.

To ensure the sub stays at the cutting-edge across the board throughout its service life, there are quick-access tech insert hatches in its design. As tech evolves during the sub's time in service, Australia can use the hatches to add the latest tech and upgrade the sub's capabilities.

RELIANT

A robot that operates underwater to protect Navy vessels and American waters from enemy mines, recently proved that it can undertake missions longer than 100 hours— that's a fair bit of endurance for a human on the trot, let alone a robot.

Reliant is an AUV — that's an Autonomous Underwater Vehicle—and this means it can undertake missions fully on its own. This robot is truly capable of working on its own and without a human equipped with a laptop and a joystick controlling its every moment, like one might expect. Created by the U.S. Naval Research Laboratory's Acoustics Division and Bluefin Robotics, Reliant recently set a record by successfully completing a 315-mile mission.

During this long-endurance challenge, Reliant operated on its own and used its heavyweight-class mine countermeasures. We hear a lot in the news about adversaries planting explosive devices on roads and land, but they also mine waters—not just land. So when U.S. forces are operating in waters with potential minefields, they need a craft designed to sense and locate the threats to help ships stay at safe distances from the mines.

That craft is often the Knifefish mine-hunter, and Reliant is a further advanced version of it.

How does it work?

The 20-foot long Reliant uses a modular design and is on the heavier side, weighing in at 1,350 pounds. When it is in the field, its subsystems can be quickly accessed so it can be rapidly maintained and turned around between missions.

For easy reconfiguration, the vehicle includes "swappable" payload sections and battery modules. To achieve that record-breaking 109-hour journey, Reliant was configured with a 40 kilowatt-hour energy section. Its high-energy capacity means it can run extended operations even at very great depths.

Reliant uses a fiber-optic gyro based inertial navigation system with GPS to navigate; it also has a Doppler velocity log for precise underwater navigation in long endurance missions.

Knifefish is based on the Bluefin 21 vehicle that can carry multiple sensors and payloads and further ramped up with a low frequency broadband sonar system. From search and salvage and oceanography through to archaeology and exploration, the Bluefin 21 is used for a range of non-military applications too.

In addition to the special Knifefish features, plans for Reliant include equipping it with two-way Iridium satellite communications, specialized sensors, and empty sections for acoustic tech like a towed receiver array.

The mission

The AUV began its 109-hour, 315-mile mission in Boston Harbor before it navigated to New York City, entirely by itself. En route, Reliant surfaced every 12.5 miles to report its position through an Iridium satellite. Human team members onshore, and aboard the M/V Matthew J. Hughes, received vehicle status information as well through the same satellite system.

In order to get the best endurance and range navigating through strong currents and busy waterways, the robot traveled at an average speed of 2.5 knots and a depth of 10 meters. Reliant travelled south past Cape Cod and then headed west, between the mainland and Martha's Vineyard, through Nantucket Sound. On the last leg, Reliant continued south of Long Island to reach its destination, making Upper New York Bay with a 10 percent energy reserve.

Next steps

This is only the first of a series of additional missions for Reliant. The tests will challenge the robot's ability to operate on its own over longer and longer missions.

As part of the Office of Naval Research Future Naval Capabilities program, the team will also be further developing Knifefish and other AUV technologies to increase mine countermeasure operational range and improve autonomy.

These sorts of advances can also be usefully applied to shallow water Anti-Submarine Warfare. It can be particularly difficult to identify bottom mines—mines that can rest on the sea floor—as well as in-volume mines that are moored. Depending on the water depth, both can be dangerous for surface vessels and both very difficult to detect. They can be especially hard to correctly and quickly find in highly cluttered environments.

Programs like Reliant and Knifefish advance technology that can help improve threat detection in these sorts of challenging environments—and by doing so, reduce risk to military vessels and personnel.

CYRO

Also designed to patrol U.S. coasts...a man-sized robot jellyfish.

Cyro is a 170 pound, highly capable robot jellyfish with military potential. A Virginia Tech College of Engineering team developed this bot prototype and he grew a whole lot in a very short span of time.

In 2012, the team led by Professor Shashank Priya first revealed RoboJelly who was the size of a real jellyfish you might come across on summer vacation or spring break. In less than a year, the team remarkably managed to evolve their jellyfish-bot from the size of a human hand to a giant jelly at nearly six feet in length.

Cyro is the product of research funded by U.S. Naval Undersea Warfare Center and the Office of Naval Research. The $5 million research program includes other universities as well such as University of California Los Angeles, the University of Texas at Dallas and Stanford University.

Military jellyfish

The goal is to create robots that are autonomous and self-powered to conduct surveillance. They could also be deployed to map ocean floors, study marine life and monitor the environment and ocean currents. UCLA's research focused on developing underwater sensing and communication for the jellyfish robots based on electric fields.

The larger the jellyfish robot, the more potential it has for greater endurance and operational range.

Why choose to base a military robot on a jellyfish? To give you a bit of context, you may want to consider this little factoid: jellyfish live in every ocean of the world, inhabiting both salt and fresh water, making it easier for a pseudo jellyfish to blend in and go undetected anywhere on the globe with water.

Compared to other marine life, jellyfish have a low metabolic rate and consume little energy, making them attractive as inspirations for robot design.

Different species of jellyfish inhabit a wide range of environments from shallow coastal waters through to more than four miles below sea level. Jellyfish are capable of enduring an equally wide spectrum of temperature.

And they also possess all sorts of surprising and interesting qualities that could be useful for military applications.

Researchers, like those at the University of Gothenburg, have been studying the North American comb jellyfish that is capable of silently approaching a target like a stealth submarine. The Nomura jellyfish can grow up to six feet long and weigh more than 600 pounds.

Jellyfish-bot

Cyro has been built to replicate the jellyfish that inspired its name, the cyanea capillata.

With a thick layer of skin made of silicone that covers the "electronic guts," Cyro is on its way to passing for a real jellyfish. Cyro is autonomous and can also swim by itself like a real one. In order to swim, the robot jellyfish has electric motors that direct its arms and artificial jelly body.

The robot jellyfish does not have a nervous system. To move and execute missions it uses "a diffused nerve net." While swimming, it can collect and analyze data at the same time. It can also relay the information back to humans.

Ultimately, the goal is for robot jellyfish to operate for months on their own. Robojelly needed to be tethered to operate, but Cyro can run on its own powered by a rechargeable nickel metal hydride battery.

In 2013, some prototypes were revealed and it looks like the robots may be capable of deployment in several years. The teams continue to work hard refining the tech in areas like reducing power consumption and improving its ability to swim. In the future, robots like this giant jellyfish could help patrol U.S. coasts to help keep Americans safe.

SEA WASP

Another jellyfish inspired robot will be a potent threat to terrorists and their underwater bombs. The autonomous Sea Wasp—robot version—looks on track to deploy and support the brave American bomb disposal teams in the not so distant future.

The sea wasp, a kind of jellyfish, can kill people in as little as three minutes by wrapping a person in ten-foot-long tentacles, inflicting stings all over the body, and injecting them with a potent and extremely painful venom.

Saab has developed technology named after this terrifying creature — in the form of a robot that will be able to discover and tackle bombs hidden underwater off U.S. shores and near American vessels.

To test its Sea Wasp tech, Saab has partnered with the Combating Terrorism Technical Support Office. The U.S. Navy Explosive Ordnance Divers Group 2, the FBI Counter-IED Section, and the South Carolina Law Enforcement Division's Counter-Terrorist Operations Maritime Response Unit are expected to be testing the Sea Wasp in 2016.

The threat

The threat of improvised explosive devices underwater continues to grow. This is a threat not just to U.S. Navy vessels, but also to commercial and civilian ships.

There has been plenty of media coverage about terrorists and other adversaries using IEDs on land, but as noted earlier they are also frequently used at sea. Just as there are minefields on land, so are their minefields in the seas—both underwater and on the surface.

By locating and defeating bombs hidden underwater, the Sea Wasp can increase safety for military, commercial and civilian vessels.

Currently, Explosive Ordnance Divers (EOD) courageously put themselves at risk to manually dispose of underwater IED threats. And since the Sea Wasp can dispose of IEDs while being operated by two people at a remote site, it creates a safe distance that reduces risk to personnel.

What does it do?

Sea Wasp is what Saab calls a Waterborne Anti-IED Security Platform. Basically, it is a robot that can travel underwater to identify and defeat bombs. And it has been specifically designed to handle the challenging conditions human EOD divers routinely face.

Sea Wasp can help protect civilians near marinas, jetties, harbors and docks as well those out in open water. Harbors and ports are attractive bomb-planting targets. This means a bomb, or bombs, might be placed in confined areas that can be tough for humans and robots to work in.

The tech is designed to tackle the tough conditions in these places and also contend with the environment of shallow depths and tidal currents. It has six thrusters powerful enough to resist 2.5 knot currents and still hover in place to evaluate and then take care of the bomb.

On the other end of things, Sea Wasp can also attach itself to structures, like a ship's hull, and operate as deep as about 200 feet underwater.

Lightweight, at less than 200 pounds, and small, at about five and a half feet long, the Sea Wasp is easily transportable and can be rapidly deployed from harbor walls, the beach and a range of boats.

IEDs are not one-size-fits-all. By definition, they are improvised and therefore can wildly vary. To handle this, the Sea Wasp comes prepared with all sorts of tools it would need to handle the range of IED form and design.

How does it work?

It only takes two humans from an EOD team to operate Sea Wasp and pilot it from the surface.

The pilots use a control console that can either be onboard the support vessel or in a vehicle on shore. The control is connected by fiber optic tether to the Sea Wasp, which is also how the robot gets its power.

To do its job, Sea Wasp is equipped with state-of-the-art sensors, including wideband sonar, LED lights and video cameras. All of these help provide Sea Wasp, and its operators, with the data necessary to defuse bombs. The sensor suite also enables them to work effectively in areas underwater where there is limited visibility.

To navigate while underwater, Sea Wasp uses high-precision tech, like its onboard Doppler Velocity Log and Internal Measurement. Using the sensor and navigation suite, Sea Wasp and its pilots find the threat that could be hidden anywhere. Next, the Sea Wasp leverages its tools and the pilots' techniques to evaluate the threat and decide on the best way to dispose of it. The pilot then uses the Sea Wasp's thrusters to lock into position on a ship's hull or wherever it needs to be to get the work done.

While this Sea Wasp does not have tentacles like its real-world namesake, it does have a very handy five-function manipulator arm. The arm has a camera attached to it that helps with examining and processing the IED. The arm also carries tools, just like a human would, to neutralize and remove the bomb.

The operator can use the manipulator arm to place a disruptor next to the explosive device.

When its job is done, the Sea Wasp is brought back to the surface where it is recovered by the team. The disruptor is then fired from the surface. It detonates, and the threat is destroyed.

UFPS

What if the U.S. could seed secret pods deep in the oceans all over the world that suddenly burst out of the water to help address an enemy threat? Wouldn't it give the U.S. Navy, and the wider military, an amazing element of surprise?

While this sounds like the stuff of science fiction, DARPA is working to make this amazing project science fact.

These pods are officially known as Upward Falling Payloads (UFPs). Hidden throughout global seas, new giant pods would let the U.S. Navy launch drones anytime, anywhere, immediately. The drones could provide critical intelligence, surveillance, reconnaissance and more to address a threat. And the pods also have the potential to release other key cutting-edge tech to support operations.

Oceans cover about 71 percent of the world's surface. The Navy needs to operate over the vastness of these oceans, yet ever-shrinking budgets continue to limit the Navy's ability to develop and acquire weapons systems and platforms.

Unmanned systems are one way to help fill these coverage gaps and to give the military the ability to strike far-flung targets. When UAVs are based on a vessel, their utility is limited by their endurance, range and the location of the vessel. With UFPs the Navy would not need to have a vessel equipped with a UAV with enough range to address a threat.

If a threat suddenly arose, then a pre-planted UFP nearby would simply need to be activated instead. It could provide immediate eyes in the sky and give a precise threat location, for example, so that the Navy could launch a missile to neutralize it.

How does it work?

UFPs look like giant 15-foot high pods or capsules. Inside is state-of-the art military technology.

When I visited the DARPA team working on them, the UFPs looked like big friendly, bright yellow capsules that could easily be mistaken for something on the set of a children's program.

Of course, UFPs will crack open to yield far more formidable surprises for adults. And their cheerful, seemingly simple exterior belies the truly extraordinary innovation involved in every aspect of the pod.

The military would pre-position these huge pods throughout the oceans. The pods would enter hibernation and could be activated after weeks, months, or years.

When needed, the military would command the UFP to "wake up." The pod would then set off on its rapid journey from ocean deep to surface using its buoyancy collar.

Once at the surface, the pod's contents are released. Inside the pod could be a small UAV that would burst forth to provide eyes in the sky. Alternatively, some speculate that the capsule could contain a futuristic weapon system that provides a decisive element in a surprise attack—but DARPA stresses the objective is not to plant weapons, but instead tech tools or even supplies to reinforce an operation. DARPA is working on a number of decisive payloads that could fit within the UFP.

What are the challenges?

There are four key elements to developing UFPs: survival in the depths for long periods of time, communicating with the pod, how the pods travel from the ocean depths to the surface and the payloads themselves—what is hidden inside the pod.

Whether on the ocean floor or in the darkest depths, the UFPs must survive under very extreme ocean pressure for very long periods of time—no small feat.

In terms of activation, communicating with something so deep under water after possibly many years of sleep is also a difficult challenge. The pod will also need to send back health status information and the military will need to be able to communicate with it from a great distance.

How does the 5,000-pound pod then rise to the surface? The UFP 'riser' is designed to provide pressure-tolerant encapsulation while rapidly rising to the surface, thanks to its collar. The collar is made out of a material that is positively buoyant so it lifts the UFP to the surface.

Once at the surface, the riser must launch its 'payload,' which could be an airborne or waterborne drone... or lots of other mind-blowing options. Some options under consideration maximize the element of surprise. The payloads could deploy for a wide range of missions including deception, decoy, disruption, situational awareness and even rescue.

How will they be used?

DARPA has been building and sea testing both the system's riser and communications components. In Phase 3, DARPA is running sea demonstrations of the UFPs communicating and rising to the surface, as well as deploying different payloads.

Almost half of the world's oceans are more than 2.5 miles deep, so if these futuristic capsules are put into use it will give the U.S. military lots of opportunities for concealment and storage of the devices. The UFPs can lie dormant and undetected for very, very long periods of time.

SMALL AND FAST

TORPEDO SEAL VEHICLE

James Bond was loaded into a torpedo tube and fired into the ocean in the 1967 film *You Only Live Twice* — and now amphibious forces can leverage far more advanced versions. Travelling via torpedo tube is just an average day at work for some in SOF.

The SEAL Pod range, available through James Fisher and Sons and James Fisher Defence Sweden, is just one version of available tech that has been made public. SEAL Pod vehicles come in three different models for different missions: Torpedo SEAL Sub SEAL and the Sea Carrier. Tested in the Stockholm archipelago, off the west coast of Scotland as well as other sites, I had the chance to look at these options while on the hunt for new, interesting SOF gear in Europe.

Although the company uses the term, SEAL, in the title, it doesn't necessarily mean that U.S. Navy SEAL teams were, or are, involved—or that they use this specific tech. But since this company's tech is public, it is a great opportunity to walk you through the types of solutions that have been developed for operators throughout the SOF spectrum, and that could be used for future missions.

Shooting forces through torpedo tubes?

The Torpedo SEAL vehicle uses a submarine torpedo tube to deploy two divers.

Stowed and carried within a NATO-standard torpedo tube, or beneath the submarine outer casing, it just needs to be extended and it is ready to use. Torpedo SEAL achieves speeds of about four knots with a lithium polymer battery and, depending on requirements, one or two thrusters.

This version is controlled by a single pilot and can carry one other warfighter and both their equipment over more than ten nautical miles when fully submerged. The Steering Information Navigation Control system gives the warfighters real time communications, sensor and location information.

Why would you shoot amphibious forces out of torpedo tubes?

This sort of vehicle could be used for a wide range of purposes. It could be used, for example, to plant explosive devices or to de-mine areas where adversaries have planted devices.

Beyond the self-evident specialized amphibious forces, the full SOF spectrum, law enforcement, counter-terrorism and border forces may also find the tech useful for operations like U.S. harbor protection and narcotics trafficking interdiction.

How about deploying forces from a submarine?

The Sub-SEAL version is larger, carries six warfighters, and can be launched from a surface craft or rotary-wing aircraft.

But it can also be deployed from underwater hangers attached to submarine casings.

Controlled by a pilot and navigator, these vehicles are operated underwater at depths of up to 30 meters. A vehicle like this would be used for missions where it is essential to stay submerged and deliver a team of six.

If necessary, it can surface to communicate or to conduct activities like reconnaissance.

Powered by lithium polymer batteries and a vectored-thruster, the Sub SEAL can sprint faster than seven knots and has a range of more than 70 km.

On the military front, it might be deployed for operations like mine countermeasures or anti-piracy, but it could also perform homeland security missions such as enforcing U.S. port protection.

SEAL Carrier

A SEAL Carrier can be launched from a surface ship and even airdropped from a medium lift helicopter or fixed-wing aircraft like a Boeing C-17.

It can also be transported by submarine, attached to the outer hull behind the sail or fin of a submarine.

One advantage the SEAL Carrier vehicle provides is that it can withstand depths of up to 150 meters — meaning more stealthy range and longer missions. This version can also carry a combat team of six and is controlled by a pilot and navigator. A smaller version, Smart SEAL, is available as well.

Capable of travelling at more than 30 knots, SEAL Carrier surface propulsion is provided by an on-board diesel engine and water-jet.

It has the option of switching to submerged mode at any point to provide a more stealthy approach. Submerged speeds are about four knots. When it is traveling submerged, an electric motor and thruster is used for propulsion.

The Carrier can also be used as a sort of base for Unmanned Underwater Vehicles—UUVs could be described in simple terms as robots that operate autonomously, as in by themselves without humans, underwater....so basically that makes it a base for smart robots that work underwater.

Get this—the Carrier can be used as a remotely operated weapons system too.

THOR Raider

What do wind farms at sea and military technology have in common? CTruk amphibious vessels.

Boatmaker CTruk, which builds wind farm service vessels, has launched a prototype craft for the military based on THOR, aka the Twin Hulled Offshore Raider.

THOR can be configured for a range of military and security tasks like assault and force transport. There are also riverine and coastal patrol options as well as a fire support configuration. THOR could deploy on tasks like mine countermeasures and interdiction to name a few.

The key here is that one vessel can take on a range of roles by being highly adaptable.

These new vessels can be extended to a length of 72 feet and feature a patented flexible pod system. The pod system means it can be re-configured in less than 8 hours. Passenger or other specialist pods can be fitted. The deckhouse can be moved to free up additional deck space.

THOR has a catamaran hull that will also form the foundation of the new military variant. Made from advanced composite materials, the company uses a resin infusion composite construction process to reduce weight and ensure an enhanced hydrodynamic shape.

For propulsion, the vessel leverages water jets. Alternative propulsion can also be fitted out.

Avenger

CTruk's Avenger is another new option available to the military and security market. A "mother ship" can carry and launch this amphibious rescue vessel capable of carrying four onboard.

Avenger can work up to approximately three miles from its mother ship accessing tough spots in shallow water, offshore sand banks and other tricky places inaccessible to most vessels at low tide.

For natural disasters, Avenger can also deploy to support humanitarian missions. It could be very useful to deliver aid and to gain access to civilians who are cut off from support due to the flooding of roads.

ZODIAC ECUME

Got an amphibious assault team that could use one helluva commando boat? Then Zodiac has been the company to go to for many, many years.

Zodiac Milpro is a legend in the business. With deep roots predating WWII, they've been innovating inflatable boats and RIBS since 1934. The company continues to be dedicated to the military market with more than 80 percent of their output for military customers.

The company works with Special Operations Forces around the world to tailor and further enhance their tech in a bespoke approach.

One example is the new boat they developed for French commandos. In Europe, I got the chance to put the new model through its paces, while getting some coaching from a Zodiac Milpro world-class coach who is also a world champion. He works closely with Special Operations Forces teams from around the world to help them sharpen their skills. It was beyond a blast learning the ins and outs of the new advances from the best, in the best. No surprise, the ECUME was impressive to say the least.

Dubbed ECUME, Zodiac designed this new boat to meet a range of mission requirements. From SOF tasks through to the protection of homeland maritime zones, this craft can tackle a whole lot of tasks.

The need for speed

ECUME is the next evolution of the popular Zodiac Hurricane ZH-935 RIB (or Rigid Hull Inflatable Boat). Its design focuses on the Special Operations need for high-speeds.

So how fast can it go? It can reach speeds that exceed 40 knots. Volvo Penta created two diesel inboard engines specifically to give this boat ultimate engine power. The aluminum air step hull's low center of gravity means that in spite of extreme ocean conditions the boat can sustain high speeds and a comfy ride no less.

The ride

Each ECUME is about several inches over 30 feet long and can carry 12 fully decked out operators.

The Zodiac Milpro MACH II (Military Air Channeled Hull) is designed to reduce water resistance and enhance directional stability. This tech means exceptional operational performance on water allowing high speeds to be maintained while improving both crew safety and fuel economy. It has a maximum cruising displacement of 7 tons.

Missions

In an assault role, the RIB can be equipped with the full array of raid weaponry and deploy on missions from Navy frigates and other vessels. It could also deploy from land to launch a raid on a target that's on the water.

And the boats can even be deployed by plane and air dropped into the war zone by a C-130 Hercules or the A400M Atlas. A singular RIB could be deployed on a mission or several could be deployed to deliver a larger assault team. ECUME is definitely capable of undertaking long-range missions.

There's even a version that can function as a small floating command post from which operators can direct a mission. ECUME is designed to carry state of the art communication systems essential for performing this role.

Protecting the shore and ports

In addition to military users, the ECUME is also a good fit for other applications like at sea rescue teams, fishery monitoring and at sea fire brigades.

The French Navy plans to leverage the speed of the ECUMEs for law enforcement patrols as well.

In 2015, French Admiral Oliver Coupry announced that the ECUME was admitted to active service with the French Navy. The French Navy had also previously adopted the Zodiac Millpro HURRICANE ZH-930. In the future, the French Navy will be leveraging fifteen ECUMEs.

ACTUV – Drone Vessel to Hunt Subs

A new surface vessel will patrol the world's oceans hunting and tracking enemy submarines—and it will execute missions without a single human being aboard.

Without a human crew, this drone vessel will be able to execute important missions independently like tracking and trailing an enemy sub over thousands of miles—not just for a day or two, or even a few weeks—this drone could hunt the enemy for months.

DARPA created the Anti-Submarine Warfare Continuous Trail Unmanned Vessel (ACTUV) program and Leidos is working with the Agency to develop the groundbreaking vessel. In 2016, DARPA unveiled the vessel during its christening.

The ACTUV enemy submarine hunter is expected to be about 130 feet long. In addition to hunting enemy subs, ACTUV will be capable of a wide range of missions, such as reconnaissance and counter-mine deployments. It could also be useful to resupply troops.

What's the threat?

The rise of tough-to-detect and track diesel electric submarines poses a significant issue the U.S. Navy increasingly will have to handle. ACTUV is designed to excel at tracking these ultra-quiet subs.

Diesel-electric submarines come at a relatively cheap price point of about $250 million. And buyers get bang for their buck. Owners, whether nation states or terrorist groups, could then gain the serious advantage of stealthy movements beneath the global ocean surfaces due to their virtually silent engines. Iran, for example, has claimed to have fleets of these sneaky subs.

How quiet is quiet? Reports suggest that some of these subs can be 15 decibels more quiet than a humpback whale.

How ACTUV will be a game changer

Enter ACTUV—who could roam the oceans for thousands and thousands of miles executing missions that would protect the U.S. from this ever growing problem.

For next level tracking, the vessel will be armed with state-of-the art sensors allowing it to detect the quietest of enemy subs. The idea is that it will be nearly impossible for a hostile sub to slip ACTUV when the unmanned vessel is on its tail.

Despite being smaller than traditional subs, ACTUV will be able to achieve speeds that exceed diesel electric propulsion submarines—and for a fraction of the cost.

ACTUV will have "logic" that allows it to not just identify other vessels, but also predict how they will behave. The sub hunter will be so smart that it should be able to interact, counter and outmaneuver manned enemy vessels.

This smart waterborne drone will offer lots of versatility, such as launching from and returning to a pier—rather than having to deploy from a ship like other UUVs. It will also give the Navy a vessel with far better endurance and be able to carry far more weight than lots of the drone surface vessels launched from ships.

As part of a team, it will be able to run operations with other unmanned vessels operating beneath the water and on the surface. The sub hunter could also work in cooperation with human teams and manned vessels too.

And get this—ACTUV is designed to figure out and comply with maritime laws, such as regulations to prevent collisions.

When ACTUV enters service, it will give the U.S. military a range of important advantages. Rather than send out a destroyer or a nuclear sub, ACTUV could be deployed, freeing up those assets and keeping costs down.

What's Next?

After the big reveal in April 2016, ACTUV will continue to be tested and refined.

NEXT IN SURFACE

FUTURE WARSHIPS

What will warships look like in thirty years?

The British Ministry of Defence and the Royal Navy challenged young scientists and engineers to design a future warship and the results may surprise you. Defense procurement specialist Startpoint released stunning images of what the futuristic ship could look like.

This cutting-edge ship concept has been dubbed Dreadnought 2050 in honor of the 1906 HMS Dreadnought, a Royal Naval battleship that eclipsed all other warships at the time.

The futuristic warship possesses many features on the wish list of militaries around the world—and some that are already underway. Dreadnought 2050 is made of advanced materials and features state of the art weapons, futuristic command center and more.

The ship's structure is made of ultra-strong acrylic composites that can be turned translucent so that crew can see through it. This means that from the Ops Room, commanders could see through the hull and watch close-in battles play out. Translucence does not translate into weakness, quite the contrary. The envisaged graphene coated acrylic hull would provide unprecedented strength.

Weapons

Dreadnought is equipped with a range of state-of-the art weapons including high-velocity torpedoes and speed-of-light weapons. The ships are equipped with 3D printers that would allow them to rapidly create weaponized and ISR drones on the fly as needed.

At the bow, Dreadnought 2050 has an electromagnetic railgun that can fire projectiles as far as long-range cruise missiles can go today. Railguns may seem the stuff of science fiction and far in the future for other maritime forces, but as we looked at earlier in the *Weapons* section, the U.S. Navy has already greatly advanced their railguns. In fact, they could be operational and ready for battle in the near future.

The futuristic vessel is also equipped with directed energy weapons to thwart incoming threats. Like railguns, directed energy weapons may indeed be in the far future for most maritime powers; however, the United States military and U.S. companies have already had great success in developing these weapons as we also saw earlier in *Weapons*. For the U.S. military, they are in the near future—rather than the stuff of science fiction that they may be for most countries.

Along the sides of the ship there are missile tubes. These tubes can launch missiles faster than Mach 5—a hypersonic speed.

In the outrigger hulls, there are torpedo tubes that fire supercavitating torpedoes that travel at more than 300 knots. Supercavitating torpedoes can travel at such tremendous speeds because they move through water in a sort of air bubble that reduces drag and friction.

Instead of a standard mast, Dreadnought 2050 has a tethered quadcopter that flies above the ship. The quadcopter is equipped with multi-spectral sensors that provide critical data. But it is also armed with a laser to take out threats like enemy aircraft, missiles and more. To provide the significant power that these capabilities require, the quadcopter's tether is made of carbon nanotubes that are cryogenically cooled.

Assault

A floodable dock, or "moon pool," is incorporated into the design so that amphibious teams like SEALs or Royal Marines can rapidly deploy. The moon pool could also be used to deploy unmanned underwater vehicles on missions like searching for explosive devices.

Above the dock there is an extendable flight deck and hangar that can be used for a fleet of weaponized drones.

A similarly-sized warship operating today would require about 200 crew, but the innovative warship would require less than half as many personnel. A current Ops Room, for example, could require 25 sailors to run it. Dreadnought 2050's Ops Room could be run by as few as five Sailors.

Command table

Dreadnought 2050 features an Ops Room with a 3-D holographic command table. The holographic image can be rotated and commanders can zoom in on specific parts of the battlefield.

From the Ops Room, five or six people can control all operations from the deepest parts of the ocean through to outer space. From underwater and sea surface through to land and air, all areas of operation can be displayed and reviewed. Crew can use smaller holographic pods to manage specific areas of operation. Real time data can be transmitted including secure voice, video or data to wherever it is needed.

Power, speed and stealth

The Dreadnought 2050 warship is powered by a fusion reactor or highly efficient turbines. The turbines drive silent electric motors to water jets. The graphene coating on the hull helps reduce drag and enhance speed. And the Dreadnought would have a low profile to ensure it is stealthy and hard to detect.

ARLEIGH BURKE-CLASS DESTROYERS

For some time, the U.S. Navy has had projects underway intended to ramp up its surface warfare capabilities and to do so invested billions of dollars in developing and building new destroyers.

DDG 51 destroyers are *Arleigh Burke*-class ships. They were commissioned in 1991 and are advanced surface combatants. The latest, named after Medal of Honor recipient Navy SEAL LT Michael Murphy, was intended to be the last DDG 51, but with the reduction in Zumwalt orders the U.S. Navy announced it would be building more *Arleigh Burke*-class destroyers. So in the future, more *Arleigh Burke*s will be joining the fleet to support surface combat requirements.

The *Arleigh Burke*-class is intended for a range of missions, from supporting carrier battle groups and amphibious groups through to anti-submarine warfare. It is also equipped to defend against a wide range of threats including ballistic missiles and submarines.

These robust 465-foot long destroyers are built to survive anything an enemy might throw at them. They leverage an all-steel construction. *Arleigh Burkes* can also take advantage of advanced missile guidance systems, advanced anti-aircraft missiles and Tomahawk missiles that can be used against enemy ships and land targets.

The *Arleigh Burke*-class can also support two Sikorsky SH-60 Seahawk helicopters. For more than two decades, the ships have continued to be upgraded, and designs for them evolve and advance, to meet Naval requirements and match evolving threats.

ZUMWALT-CLASS DESTROYERS

The new destroyers, the DDG 1000, are *Zumwalt*-class. The DDG 1000s were intended to replace the *Arleigh Burke*-class and be so ultra futuristic and advanced that they would dominate well into the future. The Navy changed its plans and orders were scaled back from thirty-two down to three. In part due to escalating costs and opinions about performance issues, *Zumwalts* became a lightening rod to controversy as well as lacerating public and media attacks.

Regardless, relentless innovation is essential to maintaining maritime superiority. The Navy aimed for the *Zumwalt* design and its new technologies to give the military unprecedented advantage. So what are the hopes for the three *Zumwalts* that are joining future Naval operations?

Similar to *Arleigh Burke*-class destroyers, the DDG 1000 is designed for a range of missions—but it has a number of key new features that set it apart. They are the biggest Destroyers ever built. In spite of the large 610-foot long size and its mammoth presence at approximately 16,000 tons, this warship is designed to be stealthy with a minimal radar signature.

The goal was for the *Zumwalt* design to take current threats like surface mines, small boats, submarine and cruise missile attacks, into consideration. Navy requirements for these ships included stealth, speed and strength. Compared to current destroyers, the *Zumwalts* are hoped to bring fifty fold more radar cross section reduction. The Navy aimed for the strike group defense capability to increase by ten fold.

General Dynamics Bath Iron Works has been building ships since 1884 so the experience and talent they bring to the project is exceptional. Bath Iron Works is the lead designer and builder of the *Arleigh Burke*-class so this is a team with a great deal of knowledge about building destroyers.

Wave piercing design

While the *Zumwalt* has been out on recent tests, locals have described mistaking the 600-foot plus destroyer for a small fishing boat. In 2016, it was announced that tests confirmed it is in fact so stealthy that it may go to sea with special reflective material to hoist in order to ensure it is more visible to other friendly ships.

So how does the biggest destroyer ever built in the fleet become so discreet that it could look like a very small boat on radar?

The *Zumwalt's* distinctive hull is called wave-piercing tumblehome. This new design slopes inward from above the waterline so it can slice through waves, improving speed and maneuverability. By reducing acoustic and infrared signatures that could be detected by enemy technology, the design enhances the destroyer's stealth.

The actual materials are important and vital to making them harder to detect as well. These destroyers will have a special composite superstructure. The advanced materials dramatically help reduce tells that an enemy would seek out. The composite superstructure will particularly help with both acoustic output and with cross section—making them harder to detect.

To further improve stealth, the *Zumwalt* reduces engine noise with a quiet, electric propulsion system. The ships are built around electric drive system in which the main engines power an electrical grid.

Futuristic weapons

Kitted out with an array of weapons, *Zumwalt*s were intended to be even more lethal with greater range and precision.

The Navy planned for the DDG 1000 to be an all-electric ship, with lots more power than the *Arleigh Burke*-class destroyers. They're expected to leverage about 78 megawatts of electricity.

How does power relate to weapons? If the ship can generate 78 megawatts, then this means potentially enough juice to bring futuristic weapons to the fight. With that much power, *Zumwalt*s can deploy directed energy weapons and the electromagnetic railgun. As we know from reviewing these weapons earlier, both are making great headway and will introduce astounding firepower to future threats.

Weapons

Until those become available, the ships' main weapons could be twin 155mm BAE Systems Advanced Gun Systems designed to fire a specialized rocket assisted guided round to attack land targets. Anti-submarine rockets as well as Tomahawk and Sea Sparrow missiles are amongst other systems that may feature on the new *Zumwalt*s as well.

The Navy aims for the *Zumwalts* to triple both naval surface fires coverage and capabilities to defeat anti-ship cruise missiles. In shallow water areas, the design is hoped to provide ten times the operating area against mines. The Navy also expects the *Zumwalts* to meet the Marine Corps' current and future fire support requirements.

Smaller Crew

While some warships may require about 300 sailors, the *Zumwalt* is so highly automated with its advanced systems that it could possibly only require about 175.

The first *Zumwalt* was delivered in 2016 and looks on track to be commissioned in October later in the year. This lead ship is named *Zumwalt* for Admiral Elmo *Zumwalt*, and carries the hull number DDG-1000. Two more *Zumwalt*-class ships, the future Michael Monsoor DDG-1001 and Lyndon B. Johnson DDG-1002, are underway in Maine.

At the time of writing, the Navy seems to have shelved plans to build a fleet of *Zumwalts*. Given the number of new *Zumwalt*-class destroyers has been reduced, the Navy has been focusing on an updated version of the *Arleigh Burke*-class destroyers and the Future Surface Combatant project.

Plans for a replacement have yet to take firm shape. The *Future Surface Combatant Study* is expected to provide some answers as to what the full set of surface combatants—including destroyers—will need to look like to combat current, evolving and future threats.

LITTORAL COMBAT SHIP

A new littoral ship that could specialize in coastal and shallow water areas is also joining the fleet. The Littoral Combat Ship (LCS) was designed to be quick and agile, and loaded with mission packages that can be configured for surface warfare, countering sea mines and anti-submarine warfare. On its maiden voyage, the Navy's first Littoral Combat Ship USS Freedom joined the 7th Fleet in the Pacific in 2013.

The first two LCS variants are the *Freedom*-class and the *Independence*. Both are slightly smaller than the U.S. Navy's guided missile frigates and have been likened to corvettes. The *Freedom* variant, built by Lockheed Martin, can reach speeds of more than 40 knots. It is just over 387 feet long with a nearly 57.8 foot beam. The displacement is approximately 3,450 MT full load. Built by General Dynamics, the *Independence* variant is longer at just over 421 feet with the beam about 104 feet. Displacement is approximately 3,200 MT full load.

The future of LCS remains far from clear. Critics have raised concerns about the cost, survivability and opinions that the ship is under-armed to name a few.

So what were the hopes for the program? The LCS can operate in both littoral waters and in open ocean. The Navy aimed for them to provide far more—perhaps as much as three times more—port access than other vessels. The design would be the key to providing this enhanced shallow water access.

Weapons

The ships can be outfitted with reconfigurable mission modules for submarine, surface or mine warfare. They were conceived, in part, to provide critical access and dominance in coastal water battlespace as well as bring enhanced lethality and survivability to the fight. Should a battle erupt, *Freedom* can act as a hub to tie together sea, air and land assets.

The LCS was designed with a view to excelling at destroying small boat threats, for example, and to support boarding operations, as another one. And the ship would have the advantage of a helicopter detachment that could comprise of an MH 60 Sea Hawk and MQ-8 Fire Scout.

Ship weapons could include ALEX decoy system, 57mm gun and .50 caliber machine guns as well as RAM and SeaRAM.

Crew

Due to the advances and automation, the ships were expected to only require a small, highly trained average crew size of about 50 with a 3:2:1 manning concept to rotate crews. In terms of the crew interfacing with the ship, the LCS was designed to have modern, advanced controls that include touch screens and joysticks.

COMBATTS-21

The ship's battle management system, made by Lockheed Martin, provides a flexible, next-generation defense system that can be reconfigured for a specific threat in days.

COMBATSS-21 is a self-defense suite and integrates radar, electro-optical infrared cameras, gunfire control system, countermeasures and short-range anti-air missiles, as well as a variety of missile and torpedo systems, naval guns and more.

Let's say the mission required weapons systems to defeat enemy subs. An anti-submarine package could include an MH-60 Romeo carrying an active dipping sonar, sonobuoys and heavy-weight torpedoes.

What if the enemy had littered the coastal waters with mines? *Freedom*'s countermeasures package is designed to search twice as quickly as earlier systems. It requires only two operators and would include tech like the Remote Multi-Mission Vehicle and Raytheon's airborne SONAR mine countermeasure detection system, AQS-20A.

Remember the USS Cole incident where American lives were lost? Small boats continue to be an ongoing threat.

To protect the fleet from this sort of asymmetric warfare, and LCS tech could include the Gun Mission Module MK 50 MOD, a Non-Line of Sight Launch System Mission Module, a MH-60R helicopter and vertical takeoff drones.

In the future, modified LCSs may be in the pipeline. What sort of additional capabilities? More firepower and more armor. Suggestions have included 25mm machine guns for close in work, torpedo decoys, anti-ship missile defense and Multi-function Towered Array detection system and more.

SAFFiR – Robot Sailors

Future surface ships will be so automated that the number of sailors necessary to man the ship will be reduced. But could things go that next step farther where robots will be joining ship crews of the future? The U.S. Navy has developed a new humanoid robot that can detect fires on a ship, withstand extreme heat up to 500 degrees, and fight a fire shoulder to shoulder with human firefighters.

The Shipboard Autonomous Firefighting Robot, known as SAFFiR, is a human-sized robot designed to join crews and fight shipboard fires at sea. Under direction and funding from the Office of Naval Research, Naval Research Laboratory researchers have been working with university researchers to develop the tech.

SAFFiR is meant to move autonomously throughout a ship, learn its layout and patrol for structural problems. The robot would be able to interact with the sailors onboard, and take on many of their dangerous fire-related tasks.

The robot continues to advance rapidly and continues to be successful in testing. At the LASR facility, controlled multi-environment and state-of-the-art labs that test out ideas before fielding them, the humanoid robots demonstrated early on how much potential they have back in 2014. Even by then, the robot was able to demonstrate complex motion, agility, and ability to walk over natural and manmade terrain—as well as handle simulated shipboard pitch and roll conditions.

The robot's artificial muscle was also showcased. The artificial muscle helped enable SAFFiR to successfully lift and activate fire suppression equipment. SAFFiR can open a water valve, lift the fire hose and walk with it and activate a nozzle—all requiring dexterity that is extremely difficult for robots.

The threat of fire

Fires at sea can be extremely dangerous with a range of challenges: the unpredictability, high temperatures and structural integrity are just a few.

On a ship, fires can pose a very serious threat to human life. Imagine you're out at sea, on a ship, and a fire breaks out several levels down and begins to rampage. The fire must be contained and put out to protect human life, but also to ensure the ship continues to be sea worthy, is ready for action and can defend itself against adversaries.

In a ship's cramped environment with lots of obstructions, firefighters must grapple with the darkness, smoke, heat and more. Stakes are high on a ship and rapid fire suppression can mean the difference between the personnel and ship surviving—or not surviving.

Should a fire get out of hand at sea, then evacuation can be a whole lot more difficult than on land. The ship's position could be out in the middle of the ocean without any other friendly ships nearby.

In the future, SAFFiR robots could allow the Navy to reduce the risk to humans as well as the damage to ships at sea. Achieving a robot that will effectively fight fires while also fitting into a ship requires a number of important advances along the way. The robot needs to "learn" and execute advanced firefighting techniques. The materials needed to make the robot must be able to withstand fire and the extreme heat. The robot will need advanced perception and the ability to navigate by itself. All of these things are not easy.

What does SAFFiR look like?

SAFFiR is about 6 feet tall, weighs approximately 150 pounds and is humanoid.

These robot firefighters can even withstand higher heat for longer periods than human firefighters — and even up to a remarkable 500 degrees Celsius. To protect robotic mechanisms and electronics from a fire's intense heat, NRL researchers developed a class of lightweight, high temperature sort of resin that stays strong while still malleable so that it can be shaped.

How does it work?

SAFFiR is no Roomba. This robot walks on legs, can change direction and even balance in the pitch and roll sea state conditions. For humans—but especially for bi-pedal robots—balancing on unstable terrain—can be extremely difficult. SAFFiR, however, can amazingly balance in rough seas, walk in all directions and even step around obstacles.

Ships are designed for humans, not robots—so for robots to inhabit a ship they need to be designed to handle a number of additional mobility challenges like sills. Wheeled robots may not be able to tackle sills, but robots that are bi-pedal (as in legs and feet like a human) could.

Using its enhanced very advanced sensors, it can do a whole range of things like detect fires and monitor the ships environment. The sensors help it to navigate the ship all by itself and to overcome obstacles it encounters. Even obstacles that humans find challenging like "knee-knocker" bulkhead openings, it can manage.

To see through smoke and detect sources of heat, it can use stereo infrared and ultraviolet cameras. When it is fighting fires, the robot would be able to wield a broad range of fire suppression tech.

It also makes sense for a robot to use the same gear as the humans. A humanoid robot could theoretically use human firefighting gear like their protective coats. Eventually, SAFFiR may even be able to handle complex "hand/eye" coordination tasks like throwing PEAT grenades. These days, most robotic programs are grappling with the challenges of getting robot to be able to open a door by itself. Even the smallest of tasks like that are very, very hard for robots so SAFFiR with all its many capabilities is already incredibly advanced.

SAFFiR is also designed to work with humans and to seamlessly integrate into human teams. Remarkably, it will understand the gestures and commands of human firefighters and respond accordingly.

What's next?

The SAFFiR prototype recently underwent successful testing aboard the decommissioned warship USS Shadwell. Eventually if SAFFIR is successful and deployed, then it could help reduce the risk to sailors and instead take on fires themselves. The robot crew members could also take on other regular tasks like scanning for corrosion and leaks, taking shipboard measurements and more. By taking on the more time-consuming tasks, they could free up human manning for other tasks.

For a robot to integrate into a human team of firefighters, the bot has to rely on advanced human-robot interaction tech. While the robot's intelligence and ability to communicate will continue to evolve, it will most likely always take orders from a human—at least in the near future.

AIR

FIGHTERS

VIPER

Flying for more than 40 years, the F-16 is world-renowned...Viper is the newest, most advanced fighter in the family. It debuted in 2015 with its maiden flight. The "Viper," F-16V, introduces numerous cutting-edge enhancements.

The F-16 can travel speeds faster than Mach 2—that's more than 1,500 mph. It is just under about fifty feet long and has a wingspan of about thirty-one feet. Made by Lockheed Martin, this 4th generation aircraft is often referred to as the Fighting Falcon.

Viper flew with Northrop Grumman's advanced APG-83 Active Electronically Scanned Array (AESA) and Northrop's Scalable Agile Beam Radar (SABR) for the first time in 2015. Northrop's SABR AESA fire control radar provides next-gen air-to-ground and air-to-air radar capability. The tech supports countering advanced threats and these AESA radars are also used by the F-22 Raptor and F-35 Lightning II.

SABR

SABR works by scanning electronically, rather than mechanically. This helps reduce the need for moving parts. The receiver, exciter, and processor functions are all contained in one replaceable unit. According to Northrop calculations, their advances produce three to five times greater reliability than current fire control radar systems.

SABR's electronically scanned beams mean faster area searches. It also means detecting and tracking earlier and identifying targets at longer ranges. All-weather targeting and situational awareness are all enhanced with the advances.

"BIG SAR" is SABR's Synthetic Aperture Radar capability for larger areas and high definition. This mode gives pilots with remarkable detail of their target areas. The digital map displays can be tailored with slew and zoom.

The tech automatically scans SAR maps to exactly locate and classify targets.

Other advances?

Viper also features a new cockpit Center Pedestal Display, a more advanced mission computer as well as other mission systems enhancements. This latest variant also gives pilots an embedded global positioning system and upgraded electronic warfare equipment. Taken all together, the tech helps give the popular aircraft even more capability.

There are more than 4,550 F-16s supporting the U.S. military and its allies.

F-35

The F-35 Lightning II Joint Strike Fighter is a 5th-generation stealth fighter designed to safely penetrate areas without advanced enemy radar seeing them — an enhanced degree of "invisibility" that the 4th generation cannot provide.

Made by Lockheed Martin, the F-35s can fly into enemy space first and attack a target at long ranges with precision weapons, clearing the way for further forces and without ever being detected.

Ultra advanced situational awareness, stealth, fighter jet speed and much, much more…this remarkably advanced, powerful, single-seat and single-engine fighter is designed to be capable of a range of missions with just one aircraft.

Stealth

So what is 5th-generation stealth? The F-35 can go where legacy aircraft cannot.

The uber-advanced stealth, called "Very Low Observable" or VLO stealth, is achieved through many advances that combine to dramatically reduce detection by enemy aircraft and air defense systems. Many of these advances are secret and rigorously protected for good reason…but here's what I can share with you.

Stealth was built into this aircraft from the very start. The 5th-generation has what is called a lower radar cross-section. The aircraft is fabricated from very advanced materials with a special coating that help the pilot fly through enemy space essentially invisible to radar.

Looking at the aircraft, it is clear that specific angles are avoided. The shape is designed in a way to reduce radar wave reflection. Further design aspects like embedded antennas and innovations to reduce heat emissions also enhance its stealth.

The stealth combined with other capabilities help an F-35 pilot to be virtually invisible to enemy aircraft and this can give the pilot the advantage of "seeing" the other aircraft first and taking action first.

VLO also plays a role in the F-35s ability to evade air defense and radars that other fighters cannot. With capabilities like state of the art stealth combined with cutting-edge electronic warfare, this will be an aircraft that can get through highly defended air spaces without ever being detected and play the important role of prosecuting targets that would have posed a threat to U.S. ground forces.

Speed

This fighter is fast. In addition to stealth, the F-35 is expected to be faster with a far greater range than previous aircraft. The F-35 can reach speeds of approximately Mach 1.6—that's about 1,199 mph. The Pratt & Whitney F135 propulsion system gives the aircraft phenomenal power. The range is about 1,450 miles.

Situational Awareness—the famous Gen III Helmet

The F-35 Gen III Helmet Mounted Display System, made by Rockwell Collins, lets pilots "see-through" their fifth-generation fighter jets. Like the aircraft, the helmet takes technology to an entirely new level and introduces a host of new capabilities.

Each state of the art helmet is tailor designed to each pilot's individual head. They are laser-scanned to fit precisely and ensure the pilot's gaze is exactly lined up with the tech. It displays all the data inside the visor that the pilot needs and also allows them to see 360 degrees.

The situational awareness that the F-35 provides is crucial and groundbreaking. Pilots are given unprecedented SA with the F-35's Helmet Mounted Display Systems. Those involved in the program have described it to me as situational awareness that is more extensive than any single-seat platform in existence.

What sort of data does the system provide? Any sort of data a pilot could need to complete a mission is available.

Targeting information airspeed, heading, altitude, warnings and more are all projected on the helmet's visor—and the data that is provided can be customized by each pilot so he, or she, gets the data they prefer and provided the way they prefer. This is truly next gen stuff compared to the traditional capability. The state-of the art helmets both reduce the pilot's workload and frees them up to enhance their responsiveness.

Throughout the airframe, there are several infrared cameras mounted. This F-35 Distributed Aperture System (DAS) streams real-time imagery from the cameras straight to the helmet. The system is so good—that when pilots look down they can "'see through" the aircraft to the ground below. If they look around, it is as if the aircraft is invisible and they can see what's outside the airframe as if it were a window.

Another key advantage is that the night vision is built right into the helmet and leverages an integrated camera.

The F-35 also possesses other fifth-generation features like integrated avionics, sensor fusion and incredibly powerful sensor packages.

Inside the cockpit, there are other advanced capabilities like speech recognition—so that a pilot can talk to an F-35 and it talks back. It also has a glass screen digital instrument panel that the pilot can touch to pull up data—sort of like operating a large, smart tablet.

How F-35A fighter pilots are harnessing high-tech 'see-through' helmets

Hill Air Force Base in Utah is home to the U.S. Air Force's first operational F-35A squadron. While learning about the new state-of-the art gear each pilot dons before getting in the cockpit of an F-35A and before I got to try it out myself...Major Jayson "Vato" Rickard of the 419th Fighter Wing let me borrow his helmet to get a feel for the capabilities and very kindly gave me his highly experienced fighter pilot's perspective on it.

So how exactly can pilots see "through" the F-35?

F-35s leverage DAS –the Distributed Aperture System. In the simplest of terms, it means that aircraft has a number of external cameras and sensors that can feed data seamlessly to the pilot. The helmet plugs into the plane, linking the helmet computer with the aircraft's. There are optical and magnetic trackers that track 360 degrees wherever the pilot points his or her head. "The cameras cover a 360-degree sphere around the aircraft so I can move my head in any direction and be able to access those sensors. Particularly useful for night-time," Rickard explained.

From a fighter pilot's perspective, what difference does the new helmet make? "It's huge for situational awareness for us ... flying at night. Most important for safety," Rickard said. "It gives me a horizon reference—when it is completely dark outside I can use those infrared cameras that tell which end is up, where the sky is, and where the ground is."

Other important features

Integrated night vision is another key advance. "We've got several cameras up here. One of them is a day vision camera and one of them is a night-vision camera, so independent of that with the DAS we talked about, with the 360 degrees and looking through [to demonstrate, he looked through the floor of the aircraft]... there's actually a camera up there that allows me to fly without night vision goggles as I would in my previous platform," he said. "So that's all built in and I can project that over my visor... this little outer visor is a sun shield and in here is where the image projects ... it's what we call the display visor."

"There's about a 30 to 40 degree image over both eyes—handy at night, but we use it extensively in the daytime for keying our weapons and maintaining situational awareness," he added.

Is it hard to use such an advanced piece of tech? "They made it very well. They made it very intuitive so cavemen fighter pilots such as myself can just plug it in and it just adds another layer of situational awareness ... so very easy to get used to, takes maybe 5 to 10 minutes of looking around before you have it figured out," said Rickard.

Looking out the window

One notable absence from the F-35A cockpit is the large piece of glass for the pilot's heads up display. But it's not missing – the heads up is integrated into the Gen III helmet. "The heads up display is actually displayed right there in my visor, so it's just completely seamless as I look at where a heads up display would be, there's a very perfect, very stable heads up display," said Rickard. "So that's a new fifth-generation improvement—we don't' actually have a heads up display as a separate piece of glass."

"Tactically, it's very useful as well because I can look out the window and find a target on the ground, I can designate and employ weapons targets on the ground or up in the air" he added. "What it really brings is my ability to look around 360 degrees and target bad guys."

Major Rickard said that the system encourages him to look around: "As fancy as our fifth-gen fighter is with all our sensors there's nothing that substitutes for looking out the window and picking out a bad guy and this display actually encourages me to do that instead of just staring inside."

Bespoke helmets

The bespoke helmet weighs about four pounds and has a great center of gravity. "This helmet is specifically built for me," said Rickard. "In fact, I sat in a scanner and they took lasers to scan my head to fit this thing so it fits me extremely well … as bulky as it looks it is actually very comfortable."

"Has to be custom built," he added. "Very critical that the helmet fits perfectly because any movement laterally, up or down, affects my ability to use the helmet sensor….[without this precise fit] the symbology wouldn't line up, I'd have a difficult time targeting stuff on the ground, stuff and in the air, so it's very critical that it's fit specifically to me."

Post-mission analysis

The Air Force will use data from the Gen III helmets for reconstructing missions. 'The reason we are the best air force in the world is because we spend hours debriefing everything," he said. "In an hour and half sortie we might spend three or four hours debriefing ... so that actually records my helmet image and allows us to reconstruct a mission ... figure out what we did right what we did wrong and develop lessons learned."

From an F-35 fighter pilot's perspective

Rickard says that F-35A will prove a critical weapon in the Air Force's arsenal. "It's absolutely where we need to go for taking the fight to the enemy, particularly in tomorrow's wars the enemy continues to get more and more advanced, the 5th generation aspects, the stealth, the sensor fusion [tech] ... is going to allow us to operate in a very contested environment, to where we will have a difficult time getting there with some of the legacy platforms like the F-16."

Weapons

Different variants may be armed differently. In 2016, the F-35 completed its first live air-to-air kill test with an AIM-9X missile from an F-35A's external wing against an aerial drone target.

In 2015, tests with a new Gatling gun were also successful. With this new gun, pilots will have the ability to engage air-to-ground and air-to-air targets. The 25mm gun is embedded into the F-35A's left wing in a way that keeps the aircraft stealthy.

Typical weapons are mounted externally, on wings for example, but the Lightning II can carry a wide weapon array including satellite-guided bombs internally.

While out at Hill Air Force Base, I had the chance to see the armament firsthand and learn more about how they were integrated and performing. The F-35As that I saw had a gun system with 181 rounds, two Guided Bomb Units and four A120 air-to-air missiles.

Electronic warfare

The aircraft's advanced electronic warfare capabilities mean it can locate and track enemy forces, jam radio frequencies and disrupt attacks—key because it means an F-35 can reach highly defended targets while suppressing enemy radar detection.

In addition to electronic warfare and air-to-air or air-to-ground attack, the F-35 could be used for invisible surveillance and reconnaissance and share the information with forces at sea and on the ground.

Three types of Lightning II

The Department of Defense's Joint Strike Fighter Program funded the F-35 program with the intention of creating an affordable next generation strike aircraft weapon systems for the Navy, Air Force and Marine Corps. It is hoped the 5th generation stealth fighter will replace several frontline aircraft.

Currently, there are three variations of the stealthy agile F-35 that could be used to defend the homeland and dominate enemy skies.

All three are supersonic, use Very Low Observable stealth and cover the spectrum of take-off needs including challenging take-off scenarios like short paved runways and aircraft carriers through to remote rudimentary roads and forward operating bases.

The F-35A Conventional Takeoff and Landing (CTOL) version carries an internal cannon and is meant for conventional runways.

The F-35B variant, designed for use by the U.S. Marine Corps, as well as the United Kingdom and Italy, has short takeoff/vertical landing (SVTOL). A very important capability, SVTOL allows it to undertake missions from small ships, ski-jump aircraft carriers or very rudimentary expeditionary airfields near front-line combat zones.

The F-35B is so smart it can land all by itself and hover at the touch of a button—even when facing stuff environmental conditions. The other variants have benefited from these advances as well.

The third version, the larger winged F-35C carrier, is designed for ultra precise handling for final ship approach. For managing the stress of catapult launches and arrested recoveries, it has a more robust structure.

Northrop Grumman, BAE Systems and Pratt & Whitney also work with Lockheed Martin on the project.

Truly a national undertaking, forty-six states and Puerto Rico involved in the F-35 program. The aircraft's modern engine delivers more than 60 percent more thrust than any other aircraft of the same weight.

Becoming combat ready

And the state-of-the art F-35s are becoming operational—meaning ready to deploy and strike well-defended targets anywhere on Earth. The Marine Corps declared their F-35Bs combat ready in 2015. The U.S. Air Force most recently declared its first squadron of fifth-generation fighter jets, the F-35A Lightning II, combat ready in August 2016. The U.S. Navy is expected to follow in the near future.

I've had the chance to visit and spend time with F-35 fighter pilots from the Marine Corps, Navy and Air Force as well as see first hand just what their aircraft will be bringing to future combat—and it is nothing short of remarkable. I got some lessons in flying the aircraft as well as the chance to wear that futuristic helmet and experience the next level situational awareness myself.

While the USAF squadron was in the final stages of putting the aircraft through its paces to declare IOC, I was invited to spend some time with the squadron and get up to speed on how the platform was performing. To reach the Initial Operational Capability milestone, the base needed at least twelve combat-ready jets capable of global deployment for missions involving basic close-air support, air interdiction, and limited suppression and destruction of enemy air defense.

The 34th Fighter Squadron of the 388th Fighter Wing, based at Hill Air Force Base, Utah, is the service's first operational F-35A squadron, having met all the established criteria for Initial Operational Capability.

USAF 388th Fighter Wing pilot Captain James Schmidt, gave me a thorough and detailed overview as we walked around the aircraft so I could get a close look at the F-

35A. Here are some of the insights from someone who flies the new aircraft.

Stealth and design

"So what makes the F-35 so unique and so effective is its stealth capabilities," Schmidt said. "And that's just one of the things that makes the F-35 unique."

Walking around the aircraft, it is immediately clear that stealth was built into this aircraft from the very start and considered in the tiniest of details. Schmidt broke down some of the stealth features.

"You notice the shape of the aircraft. You notice how the doors have angles," he said. "You'll notice the lining of the wings and how the engine is buried in a curved inlet. All of these things. The special radar absorbing material that's put on the jet— what we would call RAM— all of these things give the jet the ability able to evade modern-day radars."

"When people ask us where do we see this jet? I see this 2050 and beyond," Schmidt added. "It's the jet that we're going to need, the multirole platform to complement the F-22 and B-2 as well as we continue in today's contested environment."

Next-gen situational awareness

There has been a lot of hype surrounding the F-35's state-of-the-art helmet that allows pilots to look down and essentially "see" through the aircraft to the ground below.

From his perspective having flown the aircraft many, many times, Schmidt further explained the fundamentals of the Distributed Aperture System (DAS) and how the aircraft uses cameras and interacts with the helmet to achieve this effect.

"There are cameras all over the jet. What this does is it gives me the 360 degree of coverage....where the jet is looking outside for me," he said. "The jet takes all these cameras and it stitches them together and then it superimposes that image on the visor of my helmet. As I turn my head to look around, the cameras are looking at that one section of space but it's stitching them together so it looks like one seamless picture as I look around the jet."

And it is indeed true that the pilots can see through to the ground.

"So I could look down and it would superimpose the picture that camera is taking onto my visor," Schmidt confirmed.

So how can the aircraft carry weapons and stay stealthy?

As noted earlier, the F-35s for each service have been tailored to meet specific needs. The Air Force, for example, required a gun.

"That is the unique thing about the gun or even about the weapons... You can see that the weapons bay door are closed," Schmidt said. "That allows us to maintain our stealth ability while carrying weapons into combat. So we can carry missiles, we can carry bombs, and it's all tucked up in there, and when we need to get the weapon away or we need to prosecute a target, the doors will open, weapon away, doors will close again keeping our stealth abilities."

Cooling fire

F-35s can reach speeds of about 1,200 mph— and that requires a very powerful engine. The heat from such an engine would be a signature adversaries would try to identify.

So how can the F-35s maintain stealth?

"In addition to the Radar Absorbent Material that they have on the F-35 [there is also] a heat reducing coating or signature reducing coating material on the exhaust or the tailpipe," Schmidt explained. "How do you cool down fire? Lockheed Martin found a way to coat this with a special coating that will actually reduce the temperature of the exhaust coming out the back, which helps us fight IR threats or infrared missiles that would launch."

Flying

So what is it like to fly this fifth-generation jet? Schmidt, an experienced pilot, said, "Flying and landing this jet is amazing. It's super easy to fly. The engineers and designers of this jet wanted to make sure we could focus on what was really important, which is the tactical aspect."

He explained that the F-35A features advanced autopilot. "So if I want, I can say I want to fly at this altitude, and at this airspeed, or I want you to go from this point to this point and then I can take my hands off the controls and the jet will do exactly what I asked it to do."

The F-35A benefits from tech developed for the Navy requirements.

"So for landing— because of the Navy variant— we have this special function called Approach Power Compensator and what it does is when I'm ready to land, I get lined up on final," Schmidt revealed. "I press a button on the jet and the jet does whatever it needs to trim itself up to a perfect landing attitude so then I just fly the jet down. The jet adds power, it reduces power to change the pitch of the jet. So landing, you flare just a little bit and the jet touches down and it's done."

Schmidt described how these kinds of tech advance on the F-35 makes a difference for pilots.

"I came from another platform that was a little bit older," he said. "For me, it's amazing that they've built an aircraft that allows me to focus on the tactical aspect and not have to worry about getting to the fight or getting home from the fight. It's just a matter of focusing on what's important."

F-35B

While out at Farnborough, alongside the top brass from allied air forces around the world I had the chance to see the F-35B knock everyone's socks off including mine. It is one thing to hear about the VTOL, but it is quite another thing to see it.

Throughout the week at both RIAT (Royal International Air Tattoo) and Farnborough Air Show they put on a show that truly wowed the crowds. Even the most jaded seemed taken aback by its hovering capabilities. Discussing the aircraft with the pilots, they felt the concerns that had been raised and prevented them from a debut the previous year had been completely addressed.

In 2015, the Marine Corps announced their F-35s had reached operational status, while the Navy is aiming for 2018.

F-35C

In the summer of 2016, the U.S. Navy's F-35C headed back to the seas next for the third round of developmental tests aboard the aircraft carrier George Washington and I'm told at the time of writing on track to meet the 2018 target—in fact, it was even ahead of schedule in testing.

Joining the U.S. Navy out on the USS George Washington, I had the chance to watch carrier qualifications for the third developmental test (DT-III) phase of the F-35C. I observed the pilots run the aircraft through a broad range of elements associated with carrier suitability and integration in the at-sea environment. They were testing day and night CQs, Launch and Recovery with External Stores and Approach Handling Qualities with Symmetric and Asymmetric External Stores.

Of particular interest for me was how the Delta Flight Path or "magic carpet" would play out and the pilots I spoke to had glowing things to say about it. They were also evaluating Joint Precision Approach and Landing System, Crosswind and Maximum Weight Launches, MIL/MAX Power Launches.

The Gen III Helmet Mounted Display was thoroughly tested in night operations as well. The test provided further data on the fighter's special helmet and lighting in operations at night.

Criticism

It is important to note that the F-35 aircraft is not without its detractors. Critics cite delays and cost in the new fighter development. It is certainly true that many projects that push the envelope do not do so without hiccups along the way. And this platform has been both very expensive and not without problems.

Since the program kicked off in the early 1990s, the F-35 development has been bombarded with criticism varying from targeting it as the Pentagon's most expensive project through to concerns voiced in a Pentagon Operational Test and Evaluation Office that the fighter could not fly near thunderstorms or risk the jet's fuel tank exploding.

Cost and politics aside, I focus on what a new piece of tech can—or cannot—bring to the fight. As the biggest investment in the military portfolio, it was important to make sure to give it the time and depth accordingly in this book. Since I'm very lucky to have the privilege of directly talking to teams that develop, test and use advanced tech created for the U.S. military — not to mention seeing tests firsthand—I wanted to share with you what I've learned along the way with my access to this F-35 program.

I'm clearly passionate about this platform and believe it is vital to continue U.S. air dominance in future combat. Adversaries are indisputably nipping at the heels of F-35 capabilities keen to match, if not overmatch. Relentless innovation could not possibly be more important.

There is no question that fifth gen fighters will bring a key, crucial platform to future combat. But you don't have to take my opinion for it. I included interviews with two fighter pilots directly sharing their experienced points of view with you, and in their own words, so you could decide for yourself too. When I've spoken to four star generals through to the talented fighter pilots themselves that fly it, all of them stressed it is important and will bring exceptional next-level to the fight.

NG AIR DOMINANCE

The 5th generation F-35 Joint Strike Fighters are amidst becoming combat ready –Marine Corps declared combat ready last year, the USAF just declared in August 2016 and the Navy on track to declare soon as well...but the military recognizes it must relentlessly innovate to maintain air superiority in such a contested environment so it is already thinking about what's next.

Both the U.S. Air Force and the Navy are already window shopping and seeking sixth-generation fighters.

The question is how to ensure that the United States' next-generation, air dominance continues well into the future. What comes next after 5th gens? Both services are looking for a fighter that can dominate and take on multiple roles.

The current goal is for sixth-gen aircraft to replace the F/A-18E/F Super Hornet and EA-18G Growler aircraft. The Air Force and Navy next-gen aircraft would be ready to deploy in the 2030s.

The general pursuit goes by different, and changing, labels. But the Air Force has called its dream sixth-gen fighter the F-X and the Navy calls its pursuit of this mega advanced aircraft, the F/A-XX. Everyone is looking for air superiority well into the future and Next Generation Air Dominance. Currently, there are signals that the Air Force may be delaying while the Navy will continue to charge forward on a fighter jet solution that can be rapidly developed and built.

Northrop Grumman, and other companies like Boeing and Lockheed Martin, are developing concepts to meet this requirement. Northrop Grumman calls their sixth-generation fighter jet concept "NG Air Dominance."

When Northrop Grumman unveiled the image of their vision for the NG Air Dominance, some experts described it as similar to the B-2 bomber and others, to the X-47B drone. Moviegoers might describe the futuristic fighter jet design as a small starship that would fit right into summer blockbusters.

What can it do?

The project is shrouded in mystery and the specifications are secret, but supersonic speed, stealth and sophisticated weaponry are expected to feature in the aircraft's design. Given that NG Air Dominance is a fighter for the future, as a starting point we could expect it to leverage advanced materials, ultra high-speed processing and mega-advanced computing.

Speed

NG Air Dominance is expected to reach supersonic speeds. Supersonic is faster than the speed of sound and the speed of sound is about 760 mph at sea level static conditions. It would definitely be faster than 760.

Boeing's F/A-18E/F Super Hornet has a top speed of about 1,190 mph while the EA-18G Growler has a maximum speed of approximately 1,180 mph. Northrop's goal is for the NG Air Dominance to replace these aircraft so it could be expected to fly faster than both of these platforms as well.

The fifth gen F-35 is reaching speeds of at least 1,199 mph so a sixth gen would most likely want to deliver more speed. More speed is not impossible. It's already been done. One ultra-speedy aircraft is Lockheed Martin's state-of-the art SR-71 Blackbird. It delivered better than Mach 3 with a maximum speed of about 2,200 mph.

Laser weapons and more

NG Air Dominance is expected to carry a number of state-of-the art weapons, including laser weapons to track and destroy multiple targets.

Managing heat is important for a number of reasons including preserving—and not compromising—the stealth of the aircraft. Heat is something that could be detected by hostile forces. Power, thrust and lasers all generate heat so that's one big challenge the designers will need to overcome.

'R2D2' co-pilots?

Some reports claim that both the U.S. Navy and Air Force are looking to build next-gen fighters that don't need a human in the cockpit to fly it—these fighters would be flown by artificial intelligence (AI).

Other reports suggest that AI will serve as a co-pilot to the human pilot—kind of like how R2D2 flies as co-pilot to Luke Skywalker in the *Star Wars* movies—but one would imagine that instead of an actual robot, the AI would be seamlessly incorporated into the aircraft.

In conversations with very senior leadership, I've heard strong personal opinions expressed that the Super Hornet and Growler replacements should have unmanned capability in both ISR and strike—at the very least as an option. And that possibly the very same sixth gen platform could provide the option of a human flying it or the AI—so the same aircraft could be flown in different modes.

What does that mean in practice? If things were to head in this direction, then this could mean the U.S. military would have a sixth gen fighter that is so futuristic and "smart" it could fly itself, gather intelligence by itself, conduct reconnaissance by itself, undertake surveillance by itself and unleash strikes by itself—all without a human in the cockpit. Basically, it would be a multi-role strike fighter jet "drone."

Important to keep in mind though that with all "unmanned "platforms, there is always a "human in the loop." And although there might not be a human in the cockpit that doesn't mean that humans wouldn't be in the loop from the ground with a human acting as pilot. As Artificial Intelligence continues to rapidly advance, however, things could eventually change in future combat.

HYPERSONIC TEST VEHICLE - 3X

Lockheed Martin is also developing a Mach 6 aircraft that would be faster than any other current fighter jet.

Called the Hypersonic Test Vehicle 3X, or HTV-3X, the new plane could reach speeds of more than six times the speed of sound. That's more than seven times the typical cruising speed of the Boeing 747-8 that's been chosen as the next presidential aircraft. To give you a point of reference, the 747-8 can travel the length of three FIFA soccer fields in one second—and this aircraft would be several times faster. The HTV-3X would also far outpace anything currently flown by America's adversaries.

In 2016, Lockheed Martin Chief Executive Officer Marilyn Hewson made an announcement revealing for the first time that significant progress regarding the new fighter has been made. She explained they made several breakthroughs and were producing a controllable, low-drag, aerodynamic configuration. The HTV-3X would be capable of stable operation from take-off to sub-sonic, trans-sonic, super-sonic, and hypersonic to Mach 6.

At the time, she also noted that Lockheed plans to build and fly a demonstrator aircraft the size of an F-22. The F-22 Raptor is about 62 feet long and has a wingspan of approximately 44.5 feet. And also that Lockheed aims to prove a hypersonic aircraft can be produced at around $1 billion dollars to develop, build, and fly. While one billion is a large amount of money, in the defense world even with budget cuts U.S. defense spend is big. One billion as an initial price tag is considerably less steep that the cost of some other recent platforms.

Just how fast?

The HTV-3X would be three times faster than the F-22 Raptor fighters that have a maximum speed of about 1,500 mph. With speeds exceeding Mach 6, HTV-3X could travel the distance of the Earth's circumference in about five and half hours. To frame it a different way, it could travel the distance around the planet in about the same time it takes a typical commercial aircraft to travel from New York to Los Angeles.

X-51A

Mach 6 is astonishingly fast, but teams are also already working on achieving a truly extraordinary Mach 20. And the key may just well be an air-breathing engine. Boeing's X-51A WaveRider harnesses an air-breather and this aircraft has been making some impressive headway.

Their Silver Surfer-style, air-breathing engine defied naysayers with its triumphant recent test reaching Mach 5 — that's an astounding mile per second, or nearly 4,000 miles per hour— smashing its own previous time in flight record.

Often described as a surfboard that rides its own self-created sonic wave, the X-51A WaveRider does look sort of like the Silver Surfer's mode of travel. It's actually an unmanned scramjet-powered experimental aircraft. WaveRider weighs approximately 4,000 pounds with a fuel capacity about 270 pounds and currently has a ceiling of more than 70,000 feet.

Air breathing engines

Ordinary rocket engines tend to get their thrust from a high-pressure, high-velocity gas stream, resulting from the combustion of liquid oxidizer and a hydrogen fuel. They require on-board oxygen in a big way because they tend to use it to combust the hydrogen fuel—and this gives you speeds up to around 10,000 mph. For example, a space shuttle weighs about 165,000 pounds, but still needs to lug around an extra 1.36 million pounds of liquid oxygen.

No such albatross around the neck with these very promising air-breathing engines. The WaveRider's engine doesn't require its own oxygen supply and instead harvests the air as it flies through the atmosphere.

Due to the novel method of combustion, its current take-off doesn't look like a traditional Cape Canaveral launch. WaveRider uses a booster rocket instead to get to hypersonic speed, before the scramjet takes over and does its stuff.

Deep space exploration

The air-breathing engine that powers the X-51A WaveRider could also unlock the kind of deep-space exploration seen in popular movies and books. With air-breathing engines, future space travel could be faster and cheaper.

Astronaut pals have explained this to me in a simplified nutshell way so that I could understand and I'll share it with you. By reducing the absurdly heavy, liquid oxygen weight currently necessary to make that journey from Earth to space, cost could be reduced while speed increased. This type of engine could make possible far larger payloads and potentially revolutionize cargo transport to space—and throughout space.

On earth, some believe air breathing holds the key to ensuring the speed of U.S. military aircraft stays unmatched long into the future. Commercial air travel could also potentially become immensely accelerated — making the Concorde look positively prehistoric.

Pratt & Whitney is developing a suite of hypersonic propulsion system technologies that have defense potential well beyond aircraft. Missiles, high-speed weapons and advanced defense systems could all be enhanced by this sort of tech.

Mach 5+

In the fourth X-51A test flight for the U.S. Air Force Research Laboratory conducted in 2013, Boeing's WaveRider made the longest air-breathing, scramjet-powered hypersonic flight in history. It flew for three and a half minutes smashing its own 2010 record and reached Mach 5.1. This proof of concept test proved that it was possible to get a scram jet engine, launch it off an aircraft and the scramjet could go hypersonic. But it also proved far more than that.

How did it work? A B-52H Stratofortress released the X-51A from 50,000 feet, then a solid rocket booster accelerated the vehicle to about Mach 4.8. WaveRider jettisoned a booster and a connecting interstage. Powered by its supersonic combustion scramjet engine, it reached more than Mach 5. Having finished the mission, the X-51A made a controlled dive into the Pacific Ocean.

This fourth test produced quite the triumph. It successfully demonstrated not just the revolutionary engine, but also high temperature materials, airframe and engine integration at hypersonic speeds.

Mach 5+ vehicles by 2023?

WaveRider's recent record setting is important not just for pushing the boundaries of what's possible, but for further establishing the bedrock of the hypersonic tech of the future.

The challenges to building an aircraft like this are not small. In addition to the engine, they need to build the whole system and all with materials that can operate at hypersonic speed temperatures. The guidance system is another example of the tough advances required. They need to create guidance that can still work at faster than Mach 5 speeds—no small feat. And if humans will be onboard, then ultimately they will need to crack how humans can safely handle it.

HAWC

The U.S. Air Force and DARPA are now working together on the Hypersonic Air-breathing Weapon Concept (HAWC) program. This is a joint effort to develop technologies necessary for an air-launched hypersonic cruise missile. It would give the U.S. military a new capability to strike heavily defended and time-critical targets. Current cruise missiles, for example, travel at approximately 600 miles per hour. But the new hypersonic weapons underway could reach Mach 5 to 10—that's tremendously faster.

While a hypersonic weapons program in underway, there are also ambitions for an air-breathing aircraft for the military as well. The program could take things farther in a number of ways such as advancing hydrocarbon scramjet-powered propulsion to provide sustained hypersonic cruise. They're also looking at ways to handle the heat stresses of high-temperature cruise.

In 2015, the Air Force Chief Scientist announced the service wants to build upon the successful hypersonic test flight of the X-51 WaveRider and that together with DARPA, they plan to have a new and improved hypersonic air vehicle by as near future as 2023.

FALCON HTV-2

Although shrouded in secrecy, very interestingly it does seem like Lockheed Martin's legendary Skunk Works already may have already created a hypersonic aircraft that could travel a mind-blowing Mach 20. Dubbed Falcon HTV-2, this unmanned aircraft was launched on a rocket.

In development with DARPA, it was reported it reached speeds of 13,000 miles per hour in 2011 testing. To put this into context, if you boarded an aircraft in Los Angeles bound for New York City and you were travelling at Mach 20... instead of arriving in about five hours, you would arrive in less than 12 minutes.

This next gen, hypersonic speed could be very useful for time-critical missions and give the U.S. unprecedented speed in global strike. A Mach 20 military aircraft could be armed with state of the art weapons, it could be loaded with tech for ISR...given it is such early days, the exact extent of what it could bring to the fight remains to be seen.

It is not just about speed, it is also about the distance covered by those speeds.

The ability to conduct airstrikes against any target, anywhere in the world—and to do so at a speed far faster than adversaries is important. Even as a deterrent, the ability to strike another continent an ocean away within mere minutes would be helpful to say the least.

STEALTH BOMBERS

B-21

The new stealth bomber joining the U.S. Air Force is expected to be a remarkable aircraft. In war, this state of the art bomber could fly deep into hostile areas—undetected—where it could unleash devastating strikes against an enemy.

The future Long Range Strike Bomber has been deeply shrouded in secrecy. There certainly has been plenty of speculation about it. A Northrop Grumman commercial during the Super Bowl featured a new aircraft that at one point was literally cloaked and tantalized folks as a potential big clue. Once de-cloaked, a sort of bat wing shaped aircraft similar to the B-2 was revealed, prompting speculation that folks had seen a glimpse of the new mysterious bomber's design.

So what do we actually know about the ultra-secret stealth bomber?

The Pentagon announced that Northrop Grumman would be making the aircraft, which is intended to revolutionize stealth bombing. And in 2016, the U.S. Air Force revealed the first rendering of the concept design. The Long Range Strike Bomber looks black and its zig-zag shape is fittingly futuristic. It wouldn't look out of place in the next *Star Wars* film.

The new stealth bomber's designation is B-21, reflecting the fact it is the first bomber of the 21st century.

So what can this futuristic aircraft do?

The hope is that the new bomber will be able to launch from the U.S. and attack any spot anywhere on the globe with unrivalled stealth and lethality.

The aircraft is expected to replace the nearly four-decades-old B-1 as well as the legendary B-52 Stratofortress that has valiantly served the country for about six decades.

The military has kept details of the wish list for its new bomber classified. However, the B-21 will inevitably be fully loaded with lots of technologies and next-gen innovations. It may even withstand nuclear weapon-generated electromagnetic pulses (EMPs) and still operate.

So who is making the new bomber?

In 2016, the Pentagon revealed a few more details about the new plane. One of the key details was that Pratt & Whitney, a company that makes the F-35 engine, will build the B-21 engine.

The Air Force has also named six other companies who will help Northrop Grumman in building the rest of the bomber: BAE Systems, GKN Aerospace, Janicki Industries, Orbital ATK, Rockilowattell Collins and Spirit AeroSystems.

A chance to name the most lethal stealth bomber in the world?

For the first time, Air Force personnel were given the chance to name a revolutionary, state-of-the-art aircraft—and not just any aircraft—the chance to name the first long-range stealth bomber of the 21st century.

Air Force Secretary Deborah Lee James threw down the challenge in 2016 when she unveiled the first concept image of the bomber.

"This aircraft represents the future for our Airmen, and (their) voice is important to this process," James said. "So we have an image, we have a designation, but what we don't yet have, we don't yet have a name."

"This is where I'm challenging and I'm calling on every airman today... to give us your best suggestions for a name for the B-21, America's newest bomber," she added.

Any Airman had a shot at naming an aircraft that will fly as part of the future fleet ensuring U.S. air dominance in war for the next generation to come. The naming process closed after the three-month period in 2016 and I expect the new name will be revealed around September. Suggestions included names like Nighthawk and Ghost.

The B-21's path to creation will not be without resistance. Developing a revolutionary Long Range Strike bomber does not come at a cheap price tag. It will have to duke it out for funding against other Air Force programs and some political resistance.

If things work out, then the new bomber could start possibly deploying as early as the mid-2020s.

B-2 SPIRIT

Since the new B-21 bomber will be state of the art and intended to surpass its predecessors, we can take a look at the B-2 bomber—also made by Northrop—to get a sense of just how advanced it will be.

The B-2 Spirit Bomber (aka Stealth Bomber) aircraft has been a mainstay for the military with its stealth, long-range and big payload strike bomber capabilities.

It took its first flight in 1989 and entered the operational fleet in 1993. The original B-2 fleet was comprised of 21 aircraft.

Stealth

B-2 is built for stealth. During the Cold War, it was designed to beat air defense systems, penetrating deep into Soviet Union airspace and able to deliver a nuclear bomb if necessary. The design allows it to evade radar and makes it tough to detect. Instead of metal, the structure is made from advanced composites like resin-impregnated graphite fiber.

The four 19,000-pound-thrust F118-GE engines give the B-2 its power, allowing it to travel more than 600 miles per hour. The B-2 can fly to a ceiling of 50,000 feet and leverages a 172-foot wingspan.

The B-2 Spirit Bomber carries a crew of two and the aircraft can travel a very long range—to approximately 6,000 nautical miles. If the aircraft is refueled while in the air, then it can fly even farther—an additional 4,000 miles without landing.

This bomber can carry more than 40,000 pounds of nuclear or conventional munitions—that's the kind of armament that can dramatically change the battlespace, and the world, in one flight. The aircraft is designed to deliver these munitions precisely on target even in adverse weather conditions.

Since it was introduced more than 20 years ago, many advances have been incorporated to improve the B-2's lethality. For example, the aircraft's ability to receive updated target data while in the midst of a mission was improved. Other upgrade programs improved the B-2's capabilities to collect, process and then distribute battlefield data to teams throughout the world.

The sleek B-2 has a unique flying wing design that supports its radar evasion and hard to detect design. As the B-21 is still very early days, we can expect to see the B-2 continue to play a role in the future.

NEXT U-2

The U.S. military's U-2 surveillance plane, made by Lockheed Martin, is a legend.

The design was so outstanding and so advanced that it has been flying skies for more than half a century and continues to take on vital missions.

If the U-2 is indeed retired in 2019 and it would be a shame if it is retired, then there could be a gap in high altitude ISR (Intelligence, Surveillance and Reconnaissance) collection. Lockheed Martin's trailblazing Skunk Works, has been considering what's next.

Designs for a future next-gen ISR platform may have more endurance. It may have a low-observable body. There's been lots of speculation about what a potential next U-2 could be like in the media, but Skunk Works excels at secrecy and putting national security first—so what they have in mind to take things next level is not public. And Lockheed is one of many companies that are also considering designs for an aircraft that could replace the U-2s.

The U-2

We can take a look at the U-2 to get an idea of what could come next. Nicknamed the Dragon Lady, the U-2 is one of the longest serving aircraft in the U.S. Air Force. Like the B-52 bomber, the U-2 first took the skies for the U.S. military in the 1950s. It was designed in secret at Lockheed Martin's Skunk Works during the Cold War for important tasks like locating missile threats in Russia.

Ever since then, the aircraft has played a crucial role. According to Lockheed, the U-2 has a highly consistent mission success rate of over 95% across all Combatant Commands. The U-2 carries on a lot of highly sensitive work, but it has been said that the aircraft is on duty almost every hour of every day.

A high-altitude manned surveillance plane, it can fly twice the altitude of a commercial plane. This aircraft can conduct missions flying for 12 hours straight above 70,000 feet. The U-2 can also reach speeds of more than 475 mph.

Flying thirteen miles above the earth's surface, it can carry two and a half tons of the most advanced sensors and communications equipment in the world.

U-2 pilots have often described it to me as feeling like you're flying the edge of space and sky. In fact, the U-2 flies so high that pilots have to wear spacesuits and breathe from a special tank. Reaching such high altitudes helps to make it an extremely effective intelligence, surveillance and reconnaissance platform.

Pilots fly very long missions and sustain their energy with food especially designed for them. Because of the conditions, their food is delivered in tubes that sort of look like toothpaste tubes. I've had the chance to try quite a few and in my opinion the Key Lime Pie in particular is delicious. I've yet to meet a key lime pie on the ground nearly as good. Never ceases to impress me the kind of flavor they can pack into those tiny tubes.

HELICOPTERS

VALOR

In future combat, Valor's speed could be staggering. It could travel at twice the speed and range of conventional helicopters, more than doubling operational reach. Like the V-22 Osprey, Valor can take off like a helicopter and fly like an aircraft.

Made by Bell Helicopter, the company has been pioneering next gen state-of-the art tilt rotor tech to give the military the hoped for, next level, vertical takeoff and landing (VTOL) capabilities. The design aims to provide offer unmatched operational agility and to support the military in a range of vertical lift missions that are unachievable with current aircraft.

Valor is expected to have a top speed of about 300 knots per hour, cruising speed of 280 knots and a combat range of 500 to 800 nautical miles. The tilt rotor design gives it all that helo/aircraft versatility that the Osprey currently brings. It can carry a crew of four with fourteen troops, taking a maximum load of about 12,000 pounds.

A few times now, I've had the chance to take a very close look at the ground-breaking aircraft's prototype and there are a lot of smart choices immediately evident. The two six-foot wide side doors are a solid call for rapid boarding and dismounting. The helo incorporates state of the art countermeasures to enhance crew safety. The cabin features airborne battle boards that provide fused data and mission updates—meaning real-time tracking.

For medical evacuations, Valor can cover five times the area of current MEDEVAC helicopters. Its fuel efficiency has been improved, helping to reduce both costs and logistics burden to keep that bird fueled and ready to go.

Bell describes it as self-deployable—meaning it does not require logistical support for missions within a range of 2,100 nautical miles. Basically, the idea is more reach without reliance on transport vehicles or awkward fuel resupplies.

Valor may join the military of the future. Bell has entered the V-280 as part of the Joint Multi-Role Technology Demonstrator (JMR-TD) program. It could become part of the Army's Future Vertical Lift program that will replace the AH-64 Apaches and UH-60 Blackhawks.

This twice as fast—and twice as far—helicopter is on track for its first flight in 2017.

DEFIANT

Sikorsky Aircraft and Boeing are also working on the development of the SB-1 Defiant prototype with a view to it being in contention to replace the UH-60 Black Hawk and AH-64 Apache. The U.S. Army picked this team's design to continue development of Joint Multi-Role (JMR) high-speed rotorcraft as well.

The Defiant features a more conventional design that utilizes counter-rotating rotors and a push propeller in the helicopter's tail. It could weigh 13.6 tons and its pusher propeller give the aircraft a top speed of 250 knots. The helicopter may be able to carry four aircrew and 12 fully equipped troops.

In 2016, design was still underway so the details were yet to be confirmed and were being refined at the time of writing. Assembly was scheduled to begin by the end of the year and the Defiant team aims for the prototype to fly in 2017.

RAIDER

The new Raider helicopter, made by Sikorsky, also travels at faster speeds than conventional helicopters—a swift cruise speed of more than 230 miles per hour. The S-97 Raider has been designed to enhance combat operations with increased maneuverability, endurance, and high altitude ability.

With armed aerial scout missions in mind, the helicopter is designed to be extremely fast and agility in spite of armor and weapons. The composite airframe has a maximum gross weight of about 12,000 pounds.

The cockpit fits two pilots an in an assault configuration and Raider can also carry up to six combat-equipped troops. For armed reconnaissance, additional fuel and ammunition could be carried.

The aircraft could be capable of carrying a range of weapons like Hellfire missiles and 2.75-inch rockets, as well as .50 caliber and 7.62-mm guns. Raider has a low acoustic signature and integrated thermal management system.

Without refueling, Raider may be able to conduct missions with a range of more than 370 miles over a period of 2.7 hours on standard fuel. It can also perform well in challenging conditions, like 10,000 feet in 95 degrees Fahrenheit.

This next-gen helicopter uses Sikorsy's X2 technology. In 2010, the X2 Technology Demonstrator unofficially broke the rotorcraft speed record by travelling faster than 250 knots (288 miles per hour).

The Raider has been in development since 2010 with a view to meeting U.S. Army special operations and armed reconnaissance requirements. The first Raider flew successfully in 2015.

KING STALLION

King Stallion will be the Marine Corps' next-gen heavy lift helicopter and the goal is to give them the best heavy lift helo in the world. Ultimately, the Marine Corps plans to have eight active duty squadrons, one training squadron, and one reserve squadron.

The Marines' new helo is advanced. For starters, it will be able to lift an impressive three times more weight than its predecessor.

Also made by Sikorsky Aircraft Corporation, the CH-53K King Stallion prototype is also known by the less catchy name Engineering Development Model-1 (EDM-1). The U.S. Marine Corps' brand spanking new helicopter, completed its first flight in 2015.

What will it bring to the fight?

King Stallion will have a cruise speed of 141 knots and a range of about 530 miles.

The new helo will have similar physical dimensions as its predecessor, the CH-53E Super Stallion. It will also be powered by three engines, but with the upgraded engine power of the T408-GE-400s.

The helicopter has fourth-generation composite main rotor blades with anhedral tips and advanced airfoils. And there's also a new tail rotor head and blades. Additionally, there's an improved hydraulics and fuel system, fly-by-wire flight controls and an advanced drive system with a split torque design main gearbox.

The new helo will also introduce new features like a modern glass cockpit. The airframe structure is a new hybrid composite that will reduce both weight and vibration.

King Stallion will be capable of carrying 27,000 pounds - nearly three times the amount of its predecessor—and it will be able to carry these massive loads over 110 nautical miles under challenging "hot and high" conditions.

Lots of innovations focused on improving crew and passenger protection have also been introduced. In addition to cutting-edge self-defense weapons, the new aircraft incorporates advanced lightweight armor and enhanced ballistic protection as well. The troop seats and retracting landing gear are engineered to be crashworthy.

The Marine Corps' new helicopter will be capable of performing in the full spectrum of operating conditions while being low maintenance and highly reliable. Whether from a ship or a remote forward operating base, King Stallion can deploy in a range of conditions. The helicopter will prove handy connecting land to ship, and vice versa, for the Marine Corps.

First flight

During King Stallion's maiden flight, over the course of 30 minutes the new helo maneuvered sideways, backward and forward while hovering up to 30 feet above the ground. By 2016, the CH-53 successfully demonstrated lifting a 27,000-pound load.

VH-92A – The Next President's Helicopter

You may have heard of Air Force One, the plane that carries the United States President around the U.S. and the rest of the world...but have you heard of the President's helicopter Marine One?

The U.S. President is the highest ranking officer of the Armed Forces. The next Commander in Chief will travel in a new, next-generation helicopter.

Sikorsky Aircraft Corporation is working closely with the U.S. Navy to create the ultimate next-gen helicopter fit for the Commander in Chief. And they are getting closer and closer to making it a reality.

The "Nighthawks," the Marine Corps HMX-1 helicopter squadron, fly the presidential helo fleet. The current fleet includes VH-3Ds and VH-60Ns. Since 1957, HMX-1 has been entrusted with the important mission of ensuring that the president reaches places swiftly and safely by helicopter.

In 2014, the Navy gave Sikorsky a contract to build 21 operational helicopters and two test ones. The previous initiative to build a new helo, the VXX, for the U.S. President was abandoned due to extreme costs and delays. To help keep costs down Sikorsky is starting with the already-FAA certified S-92A aircraft as a foundation.

The company will be transforming the S-92A to meet the requirements of keeping the U.S. President safe—plus Presidential style travel—think serious ramping up.

New Helo

Known as the VH-92A, the new helo will transport the President, Vice President and other officials as necessary. A fleet, rather than just one helo, is required for a number of reasons. Decoys, for example, are flown to help keep the president safe from attack.

The details are kept secret for security reasons, but reports on the previous project suggest a range of features a world leader would require. In addition to the design ensuring it can land on the White House South Lawn, other reported specs include the ability to carry more weight and fly further without refueling.

Features like encrypted videoconferencing and other comms are necessary to enable the president to work securely during flights. And to travel safely, the aircraft would be hardened against all sorts of attacks from electromagnetic pulses (EMPs) through to missiles.

Sikorsky recently announced the acceptance of its second S-92A aircraft for the presidential helicopter replacement program. It also announced the completion of communication system integration and performance testing.

The S-92

The S-92 will be the point of departure for developing the new presidential helo. So here's what you need to know about that aircraft.

Powered by two GE CT7-8A engines, it reaches speeds of about 190 mph with a range of approximately 160 miles. The all-composite main and tail rotor blades are FAA certified for tough flight challenges like icing conditions and bird strikes.

For maximum passenger safety, the helicopter features a highly crashworthy fuel system and landing gear.

Ride fit for a President

What will it look like inside the new helicopter? The interior will be tailored as befits a U.S. President, but here's a look at some of the S-92's standard features.

The current S-92 interior can be pre-cooled or pre-heated before boarding. To get in and out of the helo, there are different door options available—VIPs often opt for the "air stair" doors.

The President could expect a very smooth ride thanks to the S-92's active vibration control tech. The cabin is spacious and, for those under six feet tall, it's comfortable to walk around in. There's also a large storage area for personal belongings.

The aim is to initially field the new helicopters in 2020 with complete fleet delivery by 2023.

KMAX – the Robot Helicopter

Robot helicopters flying missions on their own in war zones? Sound preposterous and like the stuff of future combat in movies?

Throughout combat zones, unmanned K-MAX helicopters are already used to deliver cargo and resupply troops.

This robotic helicopter has been quietly busy resupplying Marines on the battlefield and in remote locations in Afghanistan and beyond. In 2011, K-MAX became the first unmanned helicopter to fly a resupply mission, delivering approximately 3,500 pounds of cargo to Afghanistan.

The sleek looking unmanned helicopter features a design emphasizing simplicity, dropping a tail rotor to alleviate stress to the frame. The 52-foot long aircraft travels at a top speed of about 115 miles per hour, with a 48-foot wingspan.

How does it work?

While it can be flown by a human pilot, K-MAX excels at flying by itself both day and night missions. Not only is it a helicopter that can fly itself to a precise location...it is one that can fly more than 6,000 pounds of payload at sea level. It can also fly more than 4,000 pounds at a 15,000 feet density altitude.

With its four-hook carousel, resilient K-MAX can supply multiple locations in one flight and handle as much as several thousand pounds of cargo per mission.

The unmanned helicopter is the result of a partnership between Kaman Corp. and Lockheed Martin. This team combines Kaman's high-altitude, rugged, heavy-lift K-1200 airframe, with Lockheed Martin's mission management and control systems.

Why robotic helicopters?

Truck resupply convoys and their military escorts are frequently the target of improvised explosive devices and insurgent attacks. By replacing the traditional truck convoy, the unmanned K-MAX can reduce the risk to U.S. forces by thousands of hours—and by some estimates it already has. K-MAX's airdrops provide a safe, low-cost supply delivery method to get important medical equipment and food to troops.

In 2012, the aircraft performed a historic "hot hook-up," enabling personnel to attach cargo to the unmanned aircraft while in hover mode. The hot hook-up continues to be regularly used to give K-MAX cargo to carry on the return flight, further increasing its efficiency.

OPTIMUS

To grow the KMAX utility and enhance the effectiveness, the team was charged with developing a "supervised autonomy" ability, which may let the aircraft land in wind, weather and brownout conditions — and surpass the capability of human pilots in these tough conditions.

The initiative was dubbed, OPTIMUS—as in Open-Architecture Planning and Trajectory Intelligence for Managing Unmanned Systems — not a reference to Transformer Optimus Prime.

OPTIMUS gives KMAX the ability to control itself while a human maintains supervisory control. This approach also has potential for giving other unmanned aircraft this capability too—and not just K-MAX.

Firefighting back at home

In the civilian space, K-MAX also has a range of applications from helicopter logging and power line construction to ski-lift installations and even remote construction sites. The smart helo has enormous potential for emergency response missions too, ranging from firefighting and disaster relief to search and rescue. In the event a forest fire, for example, it can even lift and drop more than 24,000 pounds of water to help extinguish the fire.

ENHANCED CLASSICS

SUPER HERCULES

The U.S. military is set to expand its fleet of Super Hercules aircraft—a high-tech workhorse that mixes versatility with toughness.

The C-130J, aka Super Hercules, is the latest addition to the go-to tactical C-130 Hercules aircraft family and can deploy in tough battle situations as well as extreme environments including Antarctica. There are eleven variants of the C-130J and the C-130J is expected to replace aging C-130Es.

Compared to older C-130s, the C-130J climbs faster and higher. It also flies at a higher cruise speed than its predecessors. There's an additional fifteen feet to the fuselage in this newest model that provides more usable space. The aircraft can carry payloads upwards of 42,000 pounds.

According to creator Lockheed Martin's calculations, Super Hercules can transport 92 combat troops or 64 paratroopers—or it can handle a combination of the two up to the maximum weight. And thanks to the ultra cutting-edge tech advances, it takes less manpower for this variant.

ALLISON BARRIE

Graceful giant

Even though it is one of the biggest aircraft in operation, Super Hercules can be landed in tiny spaces from a dirt strip in the jungle to a landing strip on snow. For the snow, it can be equipped with skis. Super Hercules is fast, managing to reach speeds of 417 miles per hour with a range of over 2,000 miles. It can also climb to 28,000 feet. This latest variant, the C-130J, takes off and lands in an even shorter distance than the older models.

But this aircraft is not only transporting troops and supplies. It has also been equipped with state-of-the-art equipment that allows it to be used in special operations, armed intelligence, surveillance and reconnaissance.

Humanitarian

The Hercules is increasingly taking on missions far beyond the battlefield—delivering tens of thousands pounds of relief supplies, conducting search and rescue operations and taking part in firefighting. When deployed to fight fires, the aircraft leverages the Modular Airborne Firefighting System that can drop 3,000 gallons of water, or a fire retardant—within five seconds.

Hercules first took flight in 1954 and more than 2,400 Hercules have rolled out since then. The aircraft has supported the U.S. military for 60 years. The popular aircraft flies not just for the U.S. military, but also supports 16 other nations and 19 different operators. The Super Hercules global fleet has flown more than one million flight hours.

In 2015, the Department of Defense gave Lockheed Martin a contract to build an initial 32 of the C-130 Super Hercules. At the time of writing, it is expected this will be

208

part of a larger contract to eventually provide the military with 78 of the aircraft.

E-2D ADVANCED HAWKEYE

Dubbed "the digital quarterback," the Hawkeye E-2D gives warfighters even better awareness in the battle space and boosts airborne battle management.

Northrop Grumman's E-2D Advanced Hawkeye is the latest and most advanced E-2 Hawkeye variant and it too can provide airborne early warning command and control—boosting the U.S. Navy's capabilities even more. It will provide the Navy fleet with next-generation eyes. It can help manage missions, keep carrier battle groups out of harm's way, and sweep ahead of a strike.

This newest Hawkeye achieved initial operational capability in 2014. The Navy announced that the first operational squadron was ready to start deployment prep with E-2D Advanced Hawkeye aircraft.

The aircraft's design is unique. It has a fully integrated all-glass tactical cockpit, a rotating rotodome and a four vertical stabilizer tail configuration. Its 360-degree radar coverage provides enhanced situational awareness and all-weather tracking.

And it will provide 360-degree surveillance for American warfighters.

How is it more advanced?

The newest Hawkeye has significantly evolved since the earlier E-2 models, with the new, more powerful, AN/APY-9 radar system among its standout capabilities.

Northrop Grumman describes Hawkeye's radar technology, improved data processing, and communications as not just next generation, but a two-generation jump ahead. These advances can give warfighters the ability to see more targets at much further distances as just one example.

The new cutting-edge radar sensor capability means that warfighters can receive better data more quickly. Accelerating delivery of crucial data means the military can find out about threats and engage faster.

The radar can also operate well in a cluttered and electronically jammed war environment. Hawkeye E-2D features other advances too, such as a new mission computer and tactical workstations, as well as advanced identification friend or foe system.

How will it be used?

Hawkeye can be deployed for a range of tasks, from missile defense through to border security. It supports unprecedented response to time-critical threats.

Its excellent sensor data, battlespace situational awareness, and connectivity to other airborne assets make this "digital quarterback" ideal for coordinating air strikes against hostile targets.

From a Navy's "Sea Power 21" strategy perspective, the Advanced Hawkeye plays a role in air missile defense within the 'Sea Shield' defensive component of the strategy. And as part of 'Sea Strike,' the offensive portion of Sea Power 21, Hawkeye can provide advanced detection and tracking for operations in land and littoral, or coastal, environments.

With its open-architecture network connectivity, it can act as a FORCEnet enabler and help coordinate time-critical targeting and strike operations. FORCEnet is the naval command and control component of Sea Power 21.

Hawkeye's combined capabilities are a big advantage in defending and protecting U.S. forces in coastal areas and on land.

Well-concealed enemy launchers firing high-speed missiles that fly low with low signatures can be a threat. This type of threat often means that forces have very little reaction time once a missile breaks on the radar horizon.

For forces operating in littoral environments, safe access is crucial. The more common these advanced cruise missiles become, the more a solution like Hawkeye becomes important.

Airborne Battle Manager

Effectively an airborne battle manager, Hawkeye can operate from forward-deployed aircraft carriers.

Working with Cooperative Engagement Capability (CEC)-equipped Aegis surface combatants, Hawkeye can robustly defend against cruise missile threats. CEC is a system of hardware and software that lets Navy ships, aircraft and Marine Corps units share radar, and weapons system data, on air targets. Aegis is a centralized command-and-control and weapons control system.

With its remarkable detection capabilities, Hawkeye can be the first within the distributed missile defense network to detect a cruise missile launched from a mobile ground system.

In a scenario where adversaries suddenly gain possession of missiles, Hawkeye can detect the threat and use FORCEnet communications to notify an Aegis missile cruiser of a launched threat. Aegis then receives ongoing continuous data to help it destroy the missile.

The aircraft system can help exactly locate, and identify, an adversary's launch system. It does so by simultaneously collaborating with various assets like satellite surveillance.

Or Hawkeye can help to destroy a launcher before a second attack or after it relocates. For example, Hawkeye can be used to work closely with manned strike aircraft. Hawkeye would relay critical data to support the accuracy of their precision-guided weapons.

Hawkeye could also direct an Unmanned Aerial Vehicle (UAV).

Earlier variants of the E-2 Hawkeye have already played many essential roles in both military and humanitarian operations. They have supported the U.S. Navy as well as partners like the Japan Air Self-Defense Force and the French Navy.

In the future, more advanced Hawkeyes will be joining the military. The U.S. Navy awarded Northrop Grumman a $3.6 billion contract to deliver 25 new E-2D Advanced Hawkeye aircraft and Northrop Grumman is also building some Hawkeyes for Japan.

POSEIDON

Poseidon is the god of the sea and protector of the water domain in Greek mythology. The aircraft P-8A Poseidon was created to perform a similar role for the U.S. Navy. Based on Boeing's commercial airplane, the 737-800,

Boeing transformed this familiar modern aircraft that may have taken you on a vacation or two...into a mighty war platform.

Capable of a range of missions, Poseidon is a versatile aircraft in the U.S. Navy's arsenal. Made by Boeing, Poseidon is designed to take on the subs and surface vessels. It can also conduct missions gathering intelligence, surveillance and reconnaissance.

Eyes of the Navy

In a maritime patrol role, this aircraft can act as the eyes of the Navy fleet. Poseidon scours the world's oceans for any potential threat and can respond very quickly if a threat is spotted. It can also carry more and operate at higher altitudes than many similar aircraft—further boosting maritime patrol capabilities.

Based on Boeing's commercial aircraft, it has the fuselage of a 737-800 and the wings of a 737-900. The large plane is just shy of 130 feet long with a wingspan of just over 123 feet. It can deploy 4,500 miles from its base without refueling and can fly to heights of about 41,000 feet.

Capable of travelling 564 mph, its two engines are made by CFM International and provide about 27,000 pounds of takeoff thrust each.

The aircraft is designed to do more with less manpower. The P-8A Poseidon holds a crew of nine and can operate as an armed platform to take on targets.

Weaponry

Poseidon is armed with torpedoes and cruise missiles. Raytheon provides Poseidon's MK 54 lightweight torpedo and the AN/APY-10 radar that gives provides all weather, day and night multi-mission surveillance capabilities.

Northrop Grumman provides the aircraft's directional infrared countermeasures, its electronic support systems and data links. GE Aviation's electronics provides the plane's control system for integrated weapons. Other Poseidon partners include Spirit AeroSystems and BAE Systems.

Poseidon can also communicate with drones and harness the enhanced technology, sensors and weapons systems they can bring to the fight. While engaging an adversary, the Poseidon can also relay critical data across the military network.

The next-gen fleet

Thirty-three more Poseidon will be hitting the skies in the near future. In 2016, the U.S. Navy ordered 20 more Poseidon—this is in addition to an order for 13 more in 2015. The Royal Australian Air Force (RAAF) has been a long-time P-8A development partner with the U.S. Navy so some of these will be joining RAAF.

Ultimately, the Navy could purchase more than 100 Poseidons to replace its P-3C fleet. The P-3C Orion is a four-engine, anti-submarine and surveillance aircraft that has acted as a maritime patrol plane for about half a century.

P-8 Poseidons have operated from places like the Philippines, Japan and Singapore. In 2014, the U.S. military supported the search for the missing Malaysian Airlines flight MH370 and brought the P-8's advanced capabilities to bear on the tragedy.

SVAB – Defeating Brownouts

Current U.S. military helicopter pilots will be getting amped-up 'Superman-style' vision to help them tackle dangerous environments. One of the biggest threats to aircraft is Degraded Visual Environment or DVE and new technology made by Honeywell aims to solve this problem.

Superman's vision lets him see through things and observe high detail. Military helicopter pilots will be gaining their own version of this capability– something called Synthetic Vision Avionics Backbone. In 2016, DARPA awarded a contract to Honeywell to further develop this tech that enables helicopter pilots to deal with extreme DVE and still "see" crucial details.

Dubbed SVAB, U.S. military helicopters like the UH-60 Black Hawk will be outfitted with the Synthetic Vision Avionics Backbone for testing. Honeywell has been developing and testing it with DARPA for more than nine years.

The threat

When visibility is degraded, it can mask lurking hazards. Bad weather like rain, snow and fog can be the culprits. These conditions can cause low visibility, making it tough to land and fly.

"Brownout" is another challenge that military pilots regularly face. Their ability to see the terrain can become seriously obscured. This can particularly be a problem in the sort of desert and dry conditions that pilots regularly contend with in places like Iraq and Afghanistan.

What's a brownout? When a pilot approaches a landing zone, sand, dirt and dust can get kicked up causing degraded vision—a "brownout." Having been in my share of brownouts, it's gruesome. It can be so bad that whether you look out, down or up, all you can see is brown, brown and more brown—not a hint of the landscape you saw a moment ago.

In a brownout, the pilot loses his, or her, visual reference with the ground. The airframe can drift and collide with the ground or other structures. U.S. military pilots are massively talented and skilled—but even the most talented of pilots can find DVEs tough and this can lead to the helicopter landing hard or even rolling over.

How does it work?

Honeywell's technology provides pilots with a 3-D view of the landing zone on their flight displays. The synthetic vision system integrates data from a number of state-of-the-art sensors. Data is fused together, processed and translated into a picture of the area around the pilot.

The technology reveals to the pilots otherwise concealed dangers like other aircraft and telephone wires. In the landing zone, there could be vehicles and personnel nearby hidden in the DVE. There could also be unexpected terrain that is obscured dust.

Many companies have been trying to find a solution to DVE. Tech touted to tackle the problem includes millimeter wave radar, infrared radar, long wave and LIDAR, a laser-based surveying technology. I'd been distinctly underwhelmed with projects I'd looked at.

Defeating DVE is something I feel very strongly about and DARPA invited me to spend time with the DARPA and

Honeywell team working on SVAB. I had the chance to deep dive into the development and look at the most recent advances. In 2016, I saw firsthand SVAB was delivering astonishing results. Ultimately, military pilots could have such enhanced vision that even small holes and ditches around the landing zone will be revealed.

Cracking DVE with SVAB tech could help reduce risks to personnel. It would also yield benefits in budgets. Pentagon research estimates place the damage and loss of U.S. military aircraft due to degraded visual environments in the hundreds of millions of dollars.

Advanced military aircraft like the CH 47 F-model Chinook, AH-64 Block III Apache attack helo and the Black Hawk UH-60 M-model already give pilots enhanced support when equipped with cutting-edge moving map displays and digital flight controls. But that's no excuse not to continue to push hard to further advance in this area. Military pilots deserve the most advanced DVE defeating capabilities possible.

Honeywell continues to advance and refine the tech. As just one example, the team is updating the synthetic vision system to fuse information from DARPA's Advanced Rotary Multifunction Sensor radar, along with satellite imagery and databases of terrain and obstacles.

DVEs are a big challenge for all militaries....so armed with this technology, U.S. military pilots would have the advantage of being able to safely operate where others cannot.

AND THE OUT OF THE BOX CONCEPTS

AIRLANDER 10

The U.S. Army developed a mammoth aircraft—a hybrid of plane, helicopter, hovercraft and airship. This hybrid went civilian and in the future it may become military again.

At 302 feet, the Airlander 10 is bigger than a Boeing 747. Capable of carrying the huge amount of weight of approximately 22,050 pounds, the behemoth airship itself weighs about twice that—around 44,100 pounds.

Created by the innovative British company Hybrid Air Vehicles for the U.S. military, Airlander is a massive piece of next-gen tech can travel through the air at maximum speeds of about 80 knots per hour. The hybrid can also fly to altitudes of 20,000 feet.

Designed to meet military standards, Airlander works in extreme weather conditions and doesn't need a prepared landing zone. In fact, it can land on challenging surfaces like water, sand, snow and ice—making it an excellent option for delivering cargo to remote locations in tough conditions.

With humans on board, it can stay aloft for about five days, but when it is unmanned it can stay aloft for weeks on end. It is expected that ultimately the uber-blimps could circumnavigate the globe twice in one trip without landing.

And what's a blimp doing in a war zone with bullets whizzing around you might ask....the envelope's skin has been designed to withstand small arms fire and is made from a polymer composite of Kevlar, Mylar, and Vectran.

How does it fly?

The uber blimp hybrid combines aspects of fixed wing aircraft and helicopters with what the company calls "lighter-than-air technology."

It uses helium to get off the ground and its envelope contains 1.34 million cubic feet of helium. Helium provides about 40 percent of the total lift. There are also a total of four propellers with turbocharged V8 engines that run on diesel. Two are positioned at the back and two in the front. The Airlander leverages the fuel to help take off, land and power the propellers.

The cockpit can comfortably fit two people including the pilot in the current model.

Traditional airships have a lot of drawbacks like limited payloads, poor performance in weather variations and require lots of ground crew. The Airlander 10 has been designed to overcome all these challenges.

Army days

In 2010, Hybrid Air Vehicles began working on this Long Endurance Multi-Intelligence Vehicle (LEMV) project for the U.S. Army with team lead Northrop Grumman. The objective was to achieve a mega surveillance aircraft that could spend days in the air on a single mission. Potential uses for the vehicle included cargo transport, surveillance, and reconnaissance.

One reason the military was exploring airships is because they have the potential to carry far heavier payloads, like sensors and cameras, than some UAVs. They can also loiter and hover persistently over a specific spot.

Before budget cuts waylaid the promising project in 2013, the LEMV (aka Airlander 10) underwent test flights.

HAV purchased the project back and plans to make it available for civilian applications. It has already attracted interest from folks you might expect like oil and mining operations keen to find more efficient methods of transporting heavy cargo to remote corners of the world.

But the good news for folks is that they are considering making this military grade tech available for things like tourism—you could fly from Pole to Pole, hover over the Amazon rainforest or even spend days above Mayan ruins.

The project has recently been resuscitated with grants from the U.K. government and European Union, as well as other sources like a crowd funding campaign and private investors. And it has also attracted more unexpected interest—like Bruce Dickinson, the lead singer of Iron Maiden who has personally invested and hopes to fly it around the world.

Before RIAT in 2016, I had the chance to discuss the project in depth with the company and look at how the project had progressed. Based on what I saw and what I hear from little birds, I expect Airlander will make its maiden flight in August 2016. The company hopes Airlander 10 will find its way back to supporting the military of the future and they aim to be building 10 Airlanders a year by 2021.

AIRLANDER 50

An even larger version of the mega airship—the Airlander 50—is already in prototype. And get this—it is larger than a football field.

Airlander 50 is 390 feet long, 196 feet wide, and 115 feet tall and can carry approximately 50 passengers who can take advantage of the vehicle's all-round visibility.

Much of the tech in this version is the same—but this fella can carry a staggering 50 tons.

The airship can sort of suck itself down to the ground. It has hovercraft type capabilities with pneumatic tubes on the underside of the two outer hulls. When the flow is reversed it helps provide more stability. In flight, the system retracts and reduces drag.

The design makes it possible to get an extremely heavy payload—whether comprised of heavy lifting mining equipment or vast amounts of supplies—to remote and inaccessible corners of the world. Airlanders do not need runways and can land anywhere so that's a great advantage for responding to natural disasters or providing humanitarian support.

The company expects Airlander 50 to become available in the 2020s.

DARPA X-PLANE

The longtime hunt for the ultimate military hybrid—part helicopter, part airplane—that can conduct missions by itself may finally be over.

In the simplest of terms, the VTOL X-plane is a helicopter mash up with an airplane.

Why would the military want a mash up? Helicopters bring the ability to take off and land without an airstrip — hence VTOL, or Vertical TakeOff and Landing. This is important because it gives the military access to areas that fixed-wing aircraft can't reach. But fixed-wing aircraft provide better speed and range. And the X stands for Experimental. Taken all together you get the VTOL X-plane project.

DARPA issued a challenge to companies to create this hybrid and give it some serious X factor. The futuristic aircraft would combine the best advantages of helicopters and fixed wing together. Those capabilities would be further enhanced and surpass what is currently available on either platform.

Designed to lift massive amounts, this innovative hybrid would be smart enough to fly itself—and that's just for starters...and while it may seem the stuff of the future, the prototype is currently underway. If the initiative succeeds, then it could yield results that give the U.S. military another excellent advantage with this unprecedented capability.

Speed

The VTOL X-Plane project aims to improve top speed beyond the current 150 to 170 knots. Speed is very important. From a military perspective, faster VTOL aircraft could reduce mission times and thereby reduce the time exposed to potential enemy attack. In addition to reduced risk to personnel, it could increase the chances for successful operations.

But in addition to speed, it must also take off and land vertically and hover efficiently, all while hauling crates of cargo.

While some novel VTOL designs have increased speed, they had to compromise on other vital things like payload and range...hence DARPA challenging folks to find a solution and do better.

Competition

The intense competition was narrowed down to a final four contenders: Aurora Flight Sciences, The Boeing Company, Karem Aircraft and Sikorsky Aircraft.

The proposed designs were for an unmanned version — meaning it would fly without a human in the cockpit. But their designs and new technologies could ultimately revolutionize manned aircraft, too.

The companies also came up with designs that rely on new multipurpose technologies. Creating tech that can do more than one thing is a smart approach because it means the aircraft will need fewer systems, while reducing both the weight and space the tech requires.

For more than half a century, helicopters have been providing crucial VTOL—but the trade off is speed. Current VTOLs, like the tilt-rotor V-22 Osprey, are used operationally and give the military the option to land just about anywhere at relatively fast speeds. But the Osprey can reach only about 322 mph.

Despite the continually evolving technology, exceeding 460 mph has not worked. Some designs have managed to produce top speeds, but they have had to sacrifice payload, efficiency and range to do it. DARPA's VTOL X-X aircraft program is determined to boost top speeds without these sorts of compromises.

The X Factor of LighteningStrike

The VTOL X-plane has been an incredibly rapid paced project with DARPA already having chosen the design to move forward in 2016. The winning design went to Aurora Flight Sciences and LighteningStrike is the name of the new aircraft. The company will build a demonstrator that proves all those capabilities on DARPA's wish list.

DARPA aimed to ensure that the VTOL X-plane featured a number of impressive capabilities. It would be able to achieve a sustained flight speed of 345 to 460 mph and the hover efficiency would be at least 75 percent. It would also be able to perform useful work by carrying a lot of weight—up to 4,800 pounds. That's about 40 percent of the vehicle's projected gross weight of 10,000 to 12,000 pounds.

The lift-to-drag ratio, (or the amount of lift generated by a wing or vehicle, divided by the drag it creates by moving through the air), would also be dramatically improved.

And Aurora team's design aims to increase speed making it quicker than existing VTOL aircraft designed for comparable mission applications by approximately 50 percent.

LighteningStrike's subscale vehicle demonstrator was 20% of a full scale demonstrator and weighed 325 pounds. It was successfully flown at a U.S. military facility in 2016 and the full-scale demonstrator is expected to be completed by 2018. Phase III will produce a flight test around February 2018 so the next gen, VTOL X-plane, may even be hitting the skies for flight tests in the very near future.

THOUGHT-FLOWN FIXED-WING

Does flying a plane directed only by your thought sound implausible?

Thought-controlled flight could be arriving soon, according to the EU-funded "BrainFlight" project.

A team of scientists from the Institute for Flight System Dynamics and the Berlin Institute of Technology announced they had successfully translated brain impulses into control commands, enabling pilots in a plane simulator to achieve a range of remarkably precise maneuvers without touching the controls or pedals.

Wearing a cap with lots of cables attached, pilots in the simulator were able to land a plane simply by looking at the screen and moving the control stick with their thoughts, correcting the plane's position repeatedly until it landed.

Once it's perfected, brain-controlled flight could theoretically reduce pilot workload and increase safety. Freeing up pilots' hands would give them freedom of movement to manage other manual tasks in the cockpit.

How does it work?

To achieve the breakthrough, the researchers connected electroencephalography (EEG) electrodes to a cap to measure the pilot's brain waves. An algorithm created by Berlin Institute of Technology scientists enabled a program to decipher the brain waves and convert them into commands fed into the plane's control system.

The German team conducted its experiment using seven test subjects with a range of flight experience, including one who had no experience whatsoever.

The team reported that all seven, flying the plane only with their thoughts, managed to achieve accuracy that would meet some flying license requirements. Astonishingly, even the participants with little or no prior training succeeded in landing the planes.

One participant was able to follow eight out of ten target headings with only an incredibly small ten degree deviation. Another was able to land within only a few meters of the runway's center line. Some even managed their approach in poor visibility conditions.

Research continued into how control systems and flight dynamics must be altered to accommodate brain control. For example, pilots flying with their hands feel resistance in steering. But this sort of feedback doesn't happen in brain-controlled flying so the team began working on providing that sort of critical feedback without physical contact.

The German team's achievement isn't the first of its kind. Earlier in 2010, for example, a University of Illinois at Urbana-Champaign team announced it had flown an unmanned aircraft at a fixed altitude with the ability to adjust headings in response to the pilot's thoughts. Around the world, there have been a number of promising research projects on brain-controlled aircraft.

In 2010, British researchers revealed that fighter pilots, despite being more sensitive to irrelevant and distracting information, have significantly greater accuracy on cognitive tasks. When scientists looked at MRI scans, they found that pilots have a white matter microstructure in the right hemisphere of their brains that is different from the brains of non-pilots.

Imagine what trained military pilots might be able to do with this sort of thought-directed technology.

THOUGHT-FLOWN HELICOPTERS

What about flying a helicopter with just thought alone?

A team from the University of Minnesota has proven this is possible—but only with a small model helicopter so far. Nonetheless, they've repeatedly proven that by just using thought alone they could pilot a model helicopter through an obstacle course—and even through challenges that required quite a bit of finesse like guiding the helo through a tough series of hoops.

How does it work?

Similar to the German system, electrodes were attached to the pilot's scalp, and his brain waves were used to guide the aircraft.

Creating a mental image altered brain activity in the motor cortex and which the electrodes recorded this data. A computer program deciphered the signals and translated the pilot's intent.

Before flying, the new thought-pilots train for about ten hours—this is typically enough time for the computer to pick up the electric signals sent by the brain so that it can interpret them later, when the pilot is actually flying the drone. And it gives pilots the chance to learn techniques to clearly communicate direction with thought.

To move the helicopter in a particular direction, a user imagined clenching his or her hands. To go left, for example, the pilot pictured clenching the left hand. To go up, he clenched both hands.

Ultimately, the developers of the mind-controlled helicopter hope to adapt their technology to direct artificial limbs and other medical devices. Military helicopters are far, far more advanced than a model helo...but if this sort of tech could evolve to successfully integrate with military grade rotary wing aircraft, military pilots could truly unlock its potential for future combat.

SMART SKIN

Futuristic "smart skin" for military vehicles could allow planes, and ground vehicles, to "feel" their environment, similar to a human. The skin could let combat aircraft detect any damage by "feeling" the injury—and that's just the beginning of what it can do.

BAE Systems is developing the Smart Skin concept. The project aims to give machines the ability to 'feel' the world around them, sense and process the data like a human would and relay the information to a "brain" within the machine.

In future combat, all machines could leverage this mega-smart skin to detect things like heat, damage and stress. Combat aircraft, tanks and other land vehicles, as well as naval vessels could covered with the smart skin. Drones operating in the air, on land and at sea could also harness the technology.

How does it work?

Using a skin loaded with a range of sensors, machines could "feel" and sense things in a similar way to us. The smart skin would cover a combat aircraft — reading, recording and processing the machine's sensations.

The skin would be fully loaded with tiny computers. These very tiny computers work collaboratively to sense and understand the environment the machine moves through. The skin would also have its own power source.

Embedded in the skin are hundreds or even tens of thousands of sensors, giving the machines the ability to "sense." Called motes, some of the sensors are the size of a grain of rice, while others are the size of dust particles.

Commonly used sensor tech can often be big, cumbersome and expensive. However, smart skin has advanced tiny, highly efficient and effective multi-purpose sensors.

How would aircraft use skin?

Imagine hundreds of the tiny sensors spread across an aircraft wing. The sensors "feel" the world around them and send data back to the pilot. The sensors could sense things like wind and measure wind speed. They could also take temperature measurements.

Like human skin, smart skin would "feel" physical strain and movement. Different sensors would provide data on different things. Some sensors would measure and compute airflow while others may measure how the metal is fatiguing or under stress.

By harnessing advanced software, the sensors could communicate with each other and send signals to the pilot. After the sensory information is captured it is would be transmitted wirelessly, appearing on the pilot's display.

If something goes wrong with the "health" of the aircraft, the skin will sense it and send the data to the engineers on the ground so that as soon as it lands, they can immediately pinpoint and repair the problem.

A plane that could monitor its own health would boost safety while improving maintenance efficiency. If planes were monitoring their own health, they could also identify problems as early as possible, reducing risk to air crew.

Eventually, smart skin could be applied to machines like spraying paint.

War machines with skin that can sense and feel like an animal, or human, could certainly give the military an edge in future combat.

AIRBORNE UAV CARRIER

Could an *Avengers*-style helicarrier soon become a reality for the U.S. military?

DARPA issued a request to the public for ideas to help create aircraft-carriers in the sky.

Outreach to non-traditional contributors like this is called a Request For Information (RFI), and aims to accelerate and enhance development of cutting-edge projects. Welcoming unconventional contributors is smart way to rapidly create "leap-ahead" tech.

Rather than building a helicarrier-type craft from scratch, the initiative could focus on taking current large aircraft, like the C-130 transport plane, and transforming them into a sort of flying aircraft carrier.

Unmanned air systems, often referred to as "drones," would be carried, launched from, and land on these flying carriers.

DARPA is also interested in technologies that could potentially enhance manned and unmanned aircraft as well.

Why airborne?

So why would the military be interested in creating flying aircraft carriers?

U.S. manned aircraft are very often essential to military missions. However, deploying them means putting expensive aircraft at risk. More importantly, it also puts U.S. pilots at risk.

Dispatching small, unmanned, aircraft would reduce these risks—but many drones lack the speed, endurance and range of larger aircraft so that limits them as an effective option.

The solution? Utilize large aircraft to support the deployment of smaller unmanned ones. The larger aircraft can carry its smaller counterparts and fill this gap. They can catch a ride giving them the necessary speed, endurance and range. The unmanned aircraft could deploy from it on a range of missions, such intelligence, surveillance and reconnaissance (ISR). A flying carrier would also enable long-distance operations.

In areas where the U.S. does not have access to airfields, an *Avengers*-style flying carrier would be a fantastic option for deploying the drones in this way.

Achieving this will require lots of smart innovation, such as next-generation launch and recovery concepts for the drones.

Precision relative navigation, which is already used by the military, lets multiple aircraft coordinate flight activities. However, a real-life flying aircraft carrier that can deploy drone squadrons will likely require more advances in this area.

And rather than incur the cost and delays of starting from scratch, DARPA has proposed the very efficient approach of minimal modification to existing large aircraft.

To help deliver the ambitious DARPA program, the RFI included a request for proposals that could achieve full-system flight demonstrations—within just four years—by 2020.

UNMANNED

MICRO

MAST – Micro Drone Revolution

Several years ago, a four-minute video created by the Air Force Research Laboratory showed up on the Web and ignited enormous excitement. The video illustrated the lab's cutting-edge work on micro aerial vehicles. One of the stars was a kamikaze insect-sized drone loaded with explosives.

But drones of that level of sophistication — able to perch on telephone wires to harvest electricity or hunt down terrorists inside a building and eliminate them — still belong to the future. Or do they? Since the ARL aviary dramatic debut...things have generally been publicly quiet. Did the military abandon its ambitions for micro drones? No. So is the revolution still a foot? Yes.

Insects have been a frequent source of inspiration for the development of military micro drones. Squadrons of tiny intelligent flying and crawling robots, inspired by insects and animals, could soon roll out and help the military.

One of the most promising programs is Micro Autonomous Systems and Technology (MAST). It is the Army Research Laboratory's collaboration with a number of teams drawn from industry and academia. The 10-year initiative, which began in 2007, aims to create highly intelligent, next generation micro robots. BAE Systems is the industrial lead for the project, which also involves the NASA Jet Propulsion Lab, University of Maryland, the

University of Michigan, and the University of Pennsylvania.

Is it a wasp? Is it a spider? Is it a fly? It's actually a tiny drone conducting a military surveillance mission. The MAST-inspired micro robots could provide U.S. ground forces with an unprecedented opportunity to conduct covert surveillance within complex urban environments and very difficult terrain.

The micro-bots possess a great deal of potential for future combat. In my opinion, one of the most important things they can do is significantly increase the safety of warfighters in certain scenarios by providing eyes and ears just about anywhere.

What do they look like?

One BAE Systems prototype looks like a fly and weighs less than an ounce. Its lightweight carbon joints help the robots imitate real flies. With a wingspan of just over an inch, its wings beat 110 times per second.

One of the University of Pennsylvania's smallest robots weighs less than three quarters of an ounce and is very quick—travelling at about 53 body lengths per second.

Other tech resembles spiders, lizards and much, much more. Microbots can capitalize on their size to move quietly and undetected while blending in. They can gain access through tiny fissures and conceal themselves in teeny tiny spaces.

How could these micro robots be used?

MAST hopes to produces lots of different microbots suited to all sorts of different environments. In urban, rough or complex terrains, the microbots could be particularly useful for small units, giving them better situational awareness. The robots could be sent on missions to collect lifesaving data for frontline troops.

If a unit approaches a building and needs to know what's inside, for example, the team could deploy a reconnaissance team of microbots. The robots could penetrate a building undetected, capitalize on their size to move quietly and easily access small spaces to penetrate the most fortified of areas. From there, they can search the interior, map the layout, and provide data on weapons, bomb making materials, hostage and enemy positions, and much, much more.

Or say that a unit needs to enter an area where GPS technology won't function easily or is denied. This happens regularly underground for example. The microbots could deploy in advance to provide 3D mapping and navigation. They could also be used to detect and track people or to locate threats such as chemical and biological weapon materials.

Bot teams

The larger bots could partner with smaller bots. As a team, they will know the relative positions of their robot counterparts. The flying drones can sweep ahead, detect and relay obstacles in the path of the micro bot ground team. The flying mini-drones could detect threats located above, below, at either side and behind the microbots. Ground-based microbots would then adapt their method of movement to different terrains and react accordingly to warnings from their flying teammates.

The University of Pennsylvania has been working on giving their robots the ability to automatically reconfigure and adapt to both human commands and their environment. To ensure that these microbots can be monitored and managed as groups, the team has benn creating cutting-edge methods of sensing, communication, control and computation. The robots will be able to operate on their own and may be equipped with a range of sensors for location and orientation. They may also provide additional data from audio, thermal, magnetic, and chemical sensors.

Understanding insects

Insects and other animals have been key to developing many aspects of the micro drones. Working out how insects sense their environment, move around and react to threats is leading to breakthroughs in the bots sensing, understanding and adapting.

One of the many interesting creatures that the Army Research Laboratory has studied is the scorpion. The hairs on a scorpion's arm can sense vibrations and identify threats in its environment. Researchers want to replicate this capability, allowing a robot to detect footsteps and, if necessary, hide. The scorpion's tail system helps it change its center of motion and gravity. Scientists have also been looking at building a robot version of a scorpion's tail to give robots this capability as well.

BLACK HORNET

Black Hornet, a state of the art tiny combat drone, reported for duty this year.

Prox Dynamics PD-100 Black Hornet Block II Personal Reconnaissance System is a tiny drone helicopter that can fit into the palm of your hand. The company says it is the world's smallest operational unmanned air system.

It may look like a toy remote control helicopter on the wish list of kids young and old, but it's serious combat tech. Black Hornet is a very sophisticated military tool with three cameras tucked into a very small unit—a pretty impressive engineering feat.

On missions, the tiny drone can travel about three quarters of a mile and provide real-time live motion video back to the operator. It can also take HD photos.

Black Hornet is about four inches long and one inch wide. And this little guy is astonishingly light. It only weighs just over half an ounce—that's like the weight of three sheets of paper. The entire system, including two Black Hornets, a base station that can fit in your back pocket, a controller and a screen, weighs under three pounds.

How does it work?

This hornet does not attack. Instead, its sting comes in the form of the information it collects, all the while being extremely quiet and difficult to spot.

While it has been mostly deployed by forces in rural and rugged terrain, it can also be useful for built-up urban settings as well. Black Hornet's quiet noise profile provides a key advantage to getting very close to its target remaining undetected.

During deployments in Afghanistan, for example, the British Army has used Black Hornet to investigate terrain and locate snipers.

TERMES

Robotic crews that could build new structures on Earth or even Mars—and without human supervision?

Who would have thought the very same termites, pests that gnaw at homes throughout the United States, would be the inspiration for robots that can build new ones.

TERMES teams consist only of microbots cooperating and working with each other. A human asks them for a particular structure and they just get the job done. They don't need a foreman to get results—human or robotic.

While tiny in size, they could be big on impact.

These tiny robot construction crews could be deployed abroad to support humanitarian operations, like helping the Army Corps of Engineers build bridges and refuges. In the event of a natural disaster like Hurricane Katrina, these robots could put down sandbag barriers before the storm arrives and help rebuild buildings when it's gone.

A team of computer scientists and engineers from the Harvard School of Engineering and Applied Sciences and the Wyss Institute for Biologically Inspired Engineering has created an autonomous robotic construction crew that will be capable of doing all that and more.

The inspiration? Real termites

In Africa, millions of the tiny insects work together to build very large mounds of soil for their underground nests, facing enormous challenges over the year or so of construction. Weather conditions will erode their project and many termites will die, meaning new termites are needed to carry on for them.

Harvard's TERMES robot system is designed to mimic the behavior of termites. Like termites, the robots can build complex, three-dimensional structures without a central command or prescribed roles.

When humans build structures, they tend to have a blueprint, a plan and a foreman to direct and supervise on site.

In insect colonies, on the other hand, there is no leader to instruct the others. Termites rely on "stigmergy," where they intuitively understand how the other bugs are changing their environment and react without directly communicating.

Thanks to the Harvard team's algorithms, the TERMES robots use a sort of stigmergy, too, allowing very large groups of robots to act as a colony.

On a practical level, this means robot teams—whether it's a few robots or thousands—could deploy and accomplish the mission. As a team, they could adapt to unanticipated events all on their own still working from the same original instructions.

LOCUST

In the near future, swarms of compact flying drones could work together and execute missions autonomously.

A desert locust swarm can be 400 square miles large, 160 million strong per square mile and each locust can eat its weight in plants every day. Swarms can also travel extraordinary distances even from Africa to northern Europe — it is really no wonder locust swarms have been feared throughout history.

Just as locust swarms can dominate and devastate, so too could military drone swarms overwhelm threats and earn a reputation that equally inspires dread.

LOCUST is the U.S. Navy's Low-Cost UAV Swarming Technology program.

The Office of Naval Research recently demonstrated some of their swarm's capabilities. They launched their Coyote UAVs capable of various types of LOCUST swarm missions. Coyotes were flown into Hurricane Eduoard last summer, for example, to gather information.

Approximately three feet long, Coyote drones weigh about twelve pounds. They can fly for approximately 90 minutes and reach a maximum speed of 85 knots. After launch, Coyotes' wings unfold to fly.

LOCUST tests revealed that the drones could synchronize and execute flight formations all on their own.

How does it work?

The Navy has conducted a number of highly successful trials. In a 2016 demo with a tube based launch, drones by the dozens were fired in rapid succession out of the tube. In mid-air, the wings expanded and they hit the sky forming a formidable flock of drones.

Swarms will not be limited to launching from ships, they will also be able to launch from aircraft or large drone platforms. Tactical vehicles or ground-based installations are two further options.

LOCUST leverages big advances in how drones can share information with one another. The drones can take action autonomously working together without humans. They can collaborate and execute offensive or defensive missions.

While the drones are autonomous, the ONR stressed that humans will actively monitor missions and be on hand to step in and take control.

Why swarms?

There are a number of advantages to drone swarms beyond being expendable and reconfigurable. The Navy says that hundreds of these small UAVs could cost less than a single tactical aircraft, so lowering costs is another great advantage. By taking on missions, LOCUST could free up aircraft and personnel for other work while also reducing the risk to both personnel and to aircraft. Additionally, the swarms could also deploy to protect Marines and Sailors.

In future combat, swarms may not just hit the air, but the water too. The Navy has also developed drone boats that could swarm an enemy vessel and overwhelm it. These smart boats could leverage NASA tech that was developed for use on the Mars rover.

F-35 FIGHTER DRONE SWARMS

The U.S. Air Force is also looking into developing swarms for the fifth generation F-35 Lightening IIs. From the cockpit, F-35 fighter pilots could someday operate a swarm accompanying their aircraft. The swarms could potentially provide even more sensing, reconnaissance and targeting functions. Pilots could theoretically harness armed drones for additional weapons systems as well.

Military UAVs, like the iconic General Atomics MQ-9 Reapers and General Atomics MQ-1 Predators, are controlled by teams on the ground. If this project advances and becomes operational, then this would represent a significant shift from ground control to cockpit.

EXTENDING REACH

VECTOR HAWK

Drone in a can. The new Vector Hawk drone launches from a canister and fits in a backpack. This drone is designed to be easy to carry and rapid to launch so that when urgently needed, it can be fired off on the fly to provide eyes in the sky.

Made by Lockheed Martin, Vector Hawk will deploy to support U.S. maritime forces and can reconfigure to take on different missions.

Advantages

Vector Hawk is compact enough that it can fit into a backpack and be carried by a single warfighter. It weighs a mere four pounds and is four inches high. Its system is designed to be waterproof, making it a great choice for maritime forces.

Super quiet, it is virtually inaudible in many scenarios. Quiet is particularly handy when you need a drone that will not be detected.

In addition to launching via canister, this little fella can also be launched by hand.

Smart and autonomous, Vector Hawk can fly and land by itself. If the operator or ground station loses contact with the drone, the UAV's fail-safes kick in and ensure that it returns home or lands itself safely.

The data link features a high bandwidth software-defined radio and the mesh networking includes 3G, 4G, and LTE cellular, providing a lot of versatility for low visibility and urban operations.

Missions

Vector Hawk can reconfigure to match specific missions and warfighters can choose from four key options.

For missions that require a lot of endurance, the fixed-wing version can be deployed. Another option would be collapsible fixed-wing aircraft and this configuration could be launched from a tube or by hand.

A third option is to configure the backpackable drone for VTOL (Vertical Takeoff and Landing). Configured as tilt-rotor, Vector Hawk can VTOL and then transition into forward flight. Both of these versions can be launched from land or water surfaces.

In 2015, the Combating Terrorism Technical Support Office invested in further development of this small, versatile drone. The CTTSO identifies innovative technology that will help combat terrorism and develops it to support U.S. military operations.

MALE – Expanding at Sea

Extending reach with drones that can launch in flexible ways is not just about land. Advances are also underway to find creative ways to achieve this from the water too.

DARPA is working on a way to launch drones from a range of surface combatants. Given nearly 100 percent of the world's land area lies within about 900 nautical miles of ocean coastlines, this advance would provide strike capabilities almost anywhere in the world.

If this can be achieved, then it will also greatly increase the range for drones to provide surveillance, reconnaissance and intelligence. Independent drones that don't need bases would give the U.S. military quicker, and more flexible, reaction to hotspots.

Improving current capabilities

Airborne intelligence is a crucial asset for today's warfare. Current options include helicopters, fixed-wing aircraft and UAVs.

Fixed-wing, manned and unmanned, aircraft provide solid distance and endurance, but the problem is they require long runways or aircraft carriers. Helicopters can offer more landing and take off flexibility, but they have more distance and flight time restrictions.

MALEs are Medium-Altitude Long-Endurance drones. Today's military MALEs launch from bases on land or sometimes large ships—so their utility is limited by how they launch and recover. If MALE range could be boosted somehow, then they could provide an excellent solution.

To increase their range, DARPA reached out to industry and academia for ideas. At a Proposers' Day the Agency sought proposals to design, develop, and demonstrate a MALE UAV with a novel automated launch and recovery system that could unlock more possibilities.

In 2015, Northrop Grumman received a contract to progress the project. The goal would ultimately be to fly MALE UAVs from combatants such as the Littoral Combat Ship or destroyers. Smaller maritime UAVs, like Insitu

RQ-21 Blackjack, use pneumatic launcher and recovery systems. Instead of using a pneumatic system, the aircraft would use its own power to take off and land.

And by 2016, DARPA had already moved to the final stage in the initiative to launch MALE drones from combatants.

TERN – Lily Pad the Fleet

The Tactically Exploited Reconnaissance Node (TERN) program is named after the tern, a seabird that possesses remarkable endurance and can migrate thousands of miles every year.

TERN will give the military an additional capability to strike mobile targets anywhere in the world, at any time, around the clock. And it will give the military an easy, quick, cheap way to deploy intelligence, surveillance and reconnaissance systems.

In the joint DARPA and ONR TERN program, the MALE will be able to carry a 600-pound payload and operate 600 to 900 nautical miles from its home vessel. The launch and recovery system will fit Littoral Combat Ship 2 class ships and other surface combat vessels.

The concept has been described to me as similar to a falcon returning to the arm of any person equipped to receive it, rather than return to only its master every time. In this case, the falcon is an incredibly smart machine that doesn't need to return to its launch point and instead can lily pad around a world-class TERN equipped fleet.

One big challenge is how to design a solution that will ensure a MALE can launch from a small deck and navigate to land another small deck. Another very difficult one is how to crack the drone taking off and landing in rough seas while constrained by small decks.

TERN will need to withstand the maritime environment as well, and fit within the limited space on ships while providing endurance and carrying ability comparable to its land-launched brethren. It will also need to be designed in a way that requires minimal ship modifications.

The goal is for flight tests to begin in 2018.

XFC

How about drones that can launch from submerged submarines fired from torpedo tubes?

Sound too much like the stuff of summer blockbuster movies? Torpedo tube-fired drones are real too and have been recently achieved.

The U.S. Naval Research Laboratory with funding from ONR's Swampworks and the Department of Defense Rapid Reaction Technology Office developed this innovative approach to launching drones. Within a mere six years, this team proved it was possible. Thanks to their hard work, the Navy fired off a small drone (UAV) from a submerged sub for the first time.

Remarkably, the drone was launched with a Tomahawk missile launch canister from which it sprung up and shot out. As it deployed, its wings unfolded origami-style.

Called the XFC UAS, or eXperimental Fuel Cell Unmanned Aerial System, this drone is all-electric and fuel cell-powered. It is designed to deploy specifically from a submarine under the water.

Fully autonomous, it can perform missions for more than six hours.

How does it work?

In the initial 2013 demonstration, the XFC was fired from the torpedo tube on the USS Providence using a Sea Robin launch vehicle system. The Sea Robin launch system is designed to fit within an empty Tomahawk launch canister. With the integrated XFC, the Sea Robin launch vehicle rose to the surface where it appeared as a spar buoy.

The drone's take off system lifts it vertically out of its container so the XFC shot straight up into the air. The ultra smart, vertical launch design means that the drone could also potentially be launched from a small surface vessel or pick up truck for that matter.

The XFC then flew a mission for several hours and demonstrated real-time video streaming back to the submarine, surface support vehicles and Norfolk before landing in the Bahamas.

For the U.S. submarine force the XFC could provide very handy eyes in the sky for ISR.

EXTREME ISR AND STRIKE

PHANTOM EYE

The Phantom Eye drone can stay aloft an extraordinary four days—and when it grows up to full size it will stay aloft for a mind boggling ten days without refueling.

Created by Boeing's Phantom Works, this revolutionary aircraft is a liquid hydrogen-fueled, high altitude long endurance (HALE) unmanned aircraft system.

Hardly petite, Phantom Eye leverages a 150-foot wingspan and weighs about 9,800 pounds. The aircraft can reach heights of 65,000 feet and travel at speeds of more than 200 knots, cruising at about 150. The two 2.3-liter, four-cylinder engines give it 300 horsepower — 150 from each engine. It can carry payloads up to about 450 pounds.

Phantom Eye isn't just breaking ground from a defense perspective; it's also a very "green" aircraft. With a liquid-hydrogen propulsion system, it has excellent fuel economy. And its only by-product is water.

What can it do?

Phantom Eye could offer futuristic level on-demand, persistent intelligence, surveillance and reconnaissance. The full size is expected to stay airborne for ten days. Altitude and endurance are clear advantages for ISR. All

ALLISON BARRIE

over the world, it could also play a role with its communications and earth-sensing tech.

Testing

Its first autonomous flight was in 2012 at NASA's Dryden Flight Research Center at Edwards Air Force Base, followed a series of previous test drives on the runway.

By 2014, it was promoted to experimental status by the U.S. Air Force 412th Operations Group based on the recommendation of officials at NASA's Dryden Flight Research Center—after only just six test flights.

Having demonstrated handling and maneuverability, Boeing future test flights involve flying Phantom Eye at higher altitudes reaching more than 60,000 feet while also increasing endurance with each flight. After further demonstrator aircraft testing, a full-size operational version of Phantom Eye could be built.

When it grows up and becomes full size—not just demonstrator size—Phantom Ray may be able to stay aloft for up to ten days and carry a payload of 2,000 pounds.

Phantom Eye's ten days of unrefueled autonomous flight at 65,000 feet would introduce an unprecedented data collection advantage. The ability to persistently monitor very large areas for very long periods of time on demand will prove invaluable.

PHANTOM RAY

What if fighter aircraft could become drones as well? Phantom Ray is a jet powered fighter sized drone that is already paving the way to make that a reality.

Also created by Boeing's Phantom Works and another program shrouded in secrecy, the aircraft is evolved from the X-45C program. Phantom Works is one of the most legendary, trailblazing defense shops.

Phantom Ray could be used for ISR, but a fighter-style drone clearly has potential for strike, enemy air defense suppression, electronic attack and more. Boeing has also considered the platform for autonomous air refueling.

Testing

The remarkable drone's big first flight was April 27, 2011. On its second flight May 9, Phantom Ray reached an altitude of 7,500 feet and a speed of 178 knots. It had a clean landing after executing several maneuvers demonstrating basic air-worthiness and autonomy. Tests have been highly successful.

ECHO RANGER

Echo Ranger is also unmanned, but designed for autonomous work underwater, rather than in the sky. Like Phantom Eye and Phantom Ray, Echo Ranger hails from Boeing's Phantom Works where all sorts of cutting-edge autonomous tech gets made.

This autonomous submersible is 18.5 feet long, and in spite of weighing in at a whopping more than five tons...it can achieve speeds of eight knots. Echo Ranger can dive up to a depth of 10,000 feet and can travel as far as 80 miles without resurfacing.

Testing

On July 11, 2011, Echo Ranger dove to forty feet and then achieved its first autonomous surface exit. Afterwards, it set off and maneuvered to 400 feet on a pre-programmed course.

It can currently be configured for thirty-day missions and one of the objectives with Echo Ranger program is to achieve an amazing more than seventy days submerged.

Missions

In addition to undertaking operations abroad in enemy waters, Echo Ranger has great potential for patrolling and protecting U.S. coastline and harbors.

While it has commercial applications such as for the oil and gas industry to take high-resolution sonar images of seabeds, Echo Ranger also has promising potential for green purposes. It could detect environmental problems in the oceans and collect data including water samples for analysis for example.

ECHO SEEKER

In 2015, Boeing introduced a follow up to Echo Ranger. We can expect that its capabilities will surpass its predecessor.

As you'd imagine with state of the art, autonomous military platforms, very little detail is available for the public. What can be shared? Boeing's new unmanned underwater vehicle, Echo Seeker, is expected to perform longer missions, and at greater depths, than any other unmanned submersible.

Unprecedented autonomous military machines in the air and in the ocean do not mean that machine-on-machine warfare is around the corner... But as they continue to advance and AI continues to advance, they will definitely irrevocably change the game.

SR-72 SON OF BLACKBIRD

If the new Blackbird continues to crush it, then enemies of the U.S. could potentially look forward to hypersonic aircraft and hypersonic missiles in the not so distant future.

An unmanned aircraft, the SR-72 would fly at speeds up to Mach 6, or six times the speed of sound. At Mach 6, enemies would not have time to react—or to hide from its strike capabilities.

Recently revealed, the SR-72 project is a project of the illustrious Skunk Works of Lockheed Martin. This high-altitude drone could provide both ISR and strike. From penetrating enemy airspace through to striking locations an ocean away in less than an hour, the potential is enormous.

Lockheed has taken lessons learned from the HTV-2 program and applied them to the design of the SR-72. What sort of lessons? The HTV-2 reached speeds of Mach 20 and in doing so the advanced materials, for example, proved they were able to withstand extreme surface temperatures as hot as about 3500 degrees Fahrenheit. Lots of other research was accelerated in the HTV-2 initiative too. Hypersonic knowledge in the areas of guidance, navigation, control, aerodynamics and aerothermal effects were all greatly advanced.

The team aspires to create an aircraft that can go from a standstill to Mach 6—to do so, it will take lots of innovation in the propulsion department. The SR-72 will feature an air breathing jet engine—but not just any kind—an entirely new breed. Lockheed Martin Skunk Works has teamed up with Aerojet Rocketdyne to work together and figure out the optimum way to integrate an off-the-shelf turbine with a supersonic combustion ramjet air breathing jet engine.

Legacy

While the SR-72 looks like it will be unmanned, the SR-71 was manned.

In 1976, U.S. Air Force SR-71 Blackbird crews flew at faster than Mach 3 from New York to London in less than two hours. In 1990 when it retired, the aircraft flew from Los Angeles to Washington DC in 67 minutes. Blackbird set world records that were unbeaten for decades.

The Blackbird capabilities created forty years ago were so advanced that they are still wildly futuristic for most countries. The program was, and continues to be, protected by the utmost secrecy, but suffice it to say—it played a valuable role in national defense.

At the speed and altitudes it could achieve, even the most advanced adversaries would have had a very difficult time with their air defense systems against them. To share one tale I've heard many a time, when pilots received anti-aircraft warnings rather than prompt concern...it was laughable. Why? Because at those speeds the missiles would explode many miles away—they were far too fast to catch. Their truly futuristic capabilities rendered the most advanced air defense systems prehistoric by comparison.

The new hypersonic aircraft, dubbed SR-72 Son of the Blackbird, is expected to go twice as fast as the ultra fast SR-71.

And Lockheed Martin believes that this hypersonic aircraft is not in the distant future—the SR-72, flying the skies at Mach 6, could be operational by 2030.

Made in the USA
Middletown, DE
05 October 2016